Visions

From the Leaders of Today

For the Leaders of Tomorrow

By

Ty Boyd

VISIONS
**From the Leaders of Today
For the Leaders of Tomorrow**

Copyright ©1991 by Ty Boyd

Cover Design by Tom Crosby, Boyd-Crosby Advertising, Charlotte, N.C.

Published by ALEXA PRESS 1-800-336-2693 in conjunction with EXECUTIVE BOOKS, 1-800-233-BOOK.

1st printing, August 1991
2nd printing, September 1991
Printed in the United States of America

ACKNOWLEDGEMENTS

Few experiences in my life have exceeded the exhilaration of seeing this volume take shape and finally published.

Visions has been a team project. It bears my name, but the players who made it happen are many. When we began better than a year ago, Peg Robarchek, gifted author in her own right, began making sense from my notes, thoughts and interviews. She has proven to be 24-karat. So much of the credit for this project is rightfully hers.

Ann Wicker's countless interviews with our contributors made the details as interesting as the headlines.

My thanks to Deborah Colbert, Anne Gellman, Pat Boyd and Tom Crosby in this office. They made this dream a reality. Their force was action; mine was often only to dream.

The countless professional salespeople and accomplished management who have populated my audiences have taught me much.

Elsewhere in these pages is a list of my Board of Advisors, who have always guided me to safe waters when my adventures have taken me too close to the shallows. What friends and leaders they have been for me.

Also, heartfelt thanks to my twenty "best friends" in the speaking and training world, my associates of Speakers Roundtable. Integrity and values are their hallmark — what company in which to travel! They are listed on page 153.

I want to acknowledge the contributors who gave their time most liberally. They, too, have a great passion for the topics we've covered. I hope we have done them justice.

Finally, a father and husband humbly cherishes a sharing family. My mate and best friend Pat and our six offsprings have taught me many lessons in life. Some, herein reflected. I love you Anne, Tempe, Mimi, Robert, Eliot and Molly. Thanks to each for your special lessons. Keep on.

Ty Boyd

VISIONS
TABLE OF CONTENTS

INDEX OF LEADERS

Unless otherwise noted, all quotations from leaders were taken from personal interviews conducted for the purpose of this publication. The titles and company affiliations of the leaders in this book may have changed from the time of publication.

Hurst, Allan
Speaker and Trainer
James, Eddie
President, Bridgemon James & Shawver Adv. Inc.
Jensen, Jim
Vice President, 3-M Automotive Systems
Leonard, Stew
President, Stew Leonard Dairy Store
Linkletter, Art
Entertainer and Businessman
Mahaffey, Lloyd
President, Start Inc.
McColl, Hugh
CEO, NCNB Corporation
Mullins, Jeff
Head Basketball Coach, University of North Carolina-Charlotte
Ralston, John
Football Coach, Denver Broncos and San Francisco 49ers
Ridings, Dot
Editor, Knight-Ridder Publishing
Shaw, Dr. Ruth
President, Central Piedmont Community College
Stark, Robert
Executive Vice President, Hallmark Corporation
Sykes, John
President, Sykes Enterprises, Inc.
Tannenberg, Dieter
CEO, Sargent-Welch Scientific Company
Thoren, Don
Speaker and Management Trainer
True, Dr. Herb
Professor, Notre Dame University
Tunney, Dr. Jim
NFL Official, Professional Speaker
Yager, Dexter
Entrepreneur, Amway Executive
Yow, Kay
Women's Basektball Coach, North Carolina State University
Zimmerman, Joan
President, Southern Shows, Inc.

ABOUT THE AUTHOR

Ty Boyd began his career as a broadcaster at age 15 in his hometown of Statesville, N.C. Since that time, he has been seen and heard on nearly every television and radio station in America.

Today, Ty is better known for his second career, as one of the nation's leading business trainers and speaker. Speaking to audiences throughout the U.S. and around the world, Ty brings training in leadership, management and sales skills, as well as presentation skills. He is a charter member, past president and chairman of the National Speaker Association and has been awarded that organization's two high-

est awards — the CPAE for platform excellence and the "Oscar" of speaking, the cherished Cavett Award.

Ty is also chairman of Boyd Crosby Advertising, Inc., in Charlotte, N.C., and recently received an honorary doctorate from Lees-McRae College.

FOREWORD

Where there is no vision, the organization perishes. Goethe said, "Never let a day pass without looking at some perfect work of art, hearing some great piece of music and reading, in part, some great book." I can assure you, you are about to read a great book.

The power of a great book is in the power of a great personality. In these pages, Ty Boyd shares with us his in-depth interviews with many great personalities, their visions and lessons in leadership. Even in the title, there is a refining influence and in the index there is an outline that arouses our curiosity, stimulates interest and challenges our method.

It was said of Abraham Lincoln that he read less and thought more than anyone. This principle is absolutely essential for the leader today as it was for Lincoln in his day. Man doesn't live by bread alone. Leaders must have new ideas to excite their thinking and inspire them to action.

May these chapters constantly remind you that the best constructed piece of machinery in the world is you, that leadership is not personality, ability or title. Leadership is a price to be paid and the price begins and ends with VISION.

Charles "T" Jones

PREFACE

Hello, this is Ty Boyd.

Coming at you from the pages of a book isn't my usual style. I'm a trainer. A speaker. A TV spokesperson. So most of the time, you'll meet me at your seminars, at your annual meetings, at your conferences. Most of the time, you'll meet me face to face.

That way, I can see you nod when my message hits home or spot the questions in your eyes when I haven't quite zeroed in on the target. That way, you can see in my eyes the passion I have for my message.

Passion — that's what I have, all right. I've had a passion for communicating with people since the first day I sat down in front of a microphone and a radio control panel in Statesville, North Carolina. I was 15. I'll never forget that day. I felt the presence of my listeners. I felt the bond between us that day and every day of my years in broadcasting.

The next natural step was meeting my listeners face to face. I've been at that — speaking and training throughout the U.S. and the world — almost 25 years now. Sales rallies. Speeches. Management meetings.

But I've never lost the passion. More than 125 days every year, I pack up my best suit and step out in front of a group of business people, sales people, entrepreneurs who want to find the passion in themselves. Because they want to be the best they can be.

And I have to confess, I've learned as much from them as they've learned from me. Maybe more.

I shouldn't tell that; they'll want to start charging me for the experience.

But it's true. Everywhere I've taken my messages on being an ambassador for your company, on de-fusing the communication bomb, on collecting "moments of truth," I've come away richer. Wiser. Empowered with the knowledge others have gained through hard experience.

It is powerful knowledge, too. Knowledge from the leaders of 3-M, Aetna, Hallmark. Knowledge from the rank-and-file folks who are on the front line every day. The expertise of sales professionals who put leadership principles to work for them everyday. I've been lucky to experience the leadership of some of the greatest companies this world knows.

I'd like to share with you what I've learned. Because I believe you can benefit as much as I have, whether you're in management, in sales, in whatever arena you operate.

Whether you are a CEO with employees to motivate, a middle-manager ready to move up the next rung in the ladder, or a freshly minted MBA with much to prove, you can grow from the knowledge I've brought home from the world's great business leaders. Whether you are the top sales professional in your organization, or the newcomer who's still wondering how you'll meet your quota, you can grow using these principles.

You — and the people who report to you or work in the office next to you — can learn what sets these great leaders apart from the crowd. What's contributed to their success. What's made their companies great.

And most of all, what they feel it's going to take to keep them great through the decade ahead. Into the new century ahead.

Hard to believe, isn't it, that we've got so little time before we move into the 21st Century?

Will you be ready for what it brings? Will you have the skills, the insight, the flexibility necessary to challenge the new century we're moving toward so quickly?

You will, if you understand the changes we'll see in the workplace during this decade. You will, if you are courageous enough to become a new kind of leader. A leader who isn't afraid to add one word to your list of credentials.

One word: Ethics.

Ethics. Now, that's not something we've been accustomed to hearing much about in the past few decades. We're business people. It's a dog-eat-dog world. Right? Everybody pads their expense accounts. Right? You scratch my back and I'll scratch yours. Right? As long as the IRS doesn't catch you at it, it doesn't count.

Maybe that's worked in the past. Maybe it even works today. Sometimes. But it's not going to work for long.

It won't work tomorrow. It won't find new members of the team among your co-workers.

It won't keep those same people pulling for the same goals. It won't keep clients loyal. It won't encourage the kind of innovative, creating thinking you'll need to ride the crest of accomplishment. It won't earn you the reputation for being a high-performance individual.

And it won't even help you keep the fire burning in your own belly. The fire that makes each day a challenge to be relished, an opportunity to anticipate with enthusiasm.

Ethics. Values. Integrity. Americans are demanding those things of their leaders.

Those things need to color every decision, every action you make as a leader in the decade to come. I'm going to tell you why. And how.

This book is more than Ty Boyd reporting to you about what you need to do. Think of it as your guide to establishing the set of rules you'll need to become — and remain — a leader for the 21st Century. You'll be guided, not just by Ty, but by some of the finest leaders of business, public service, sales and athletics that this nation knows.

As I said before, I usually find myself talking to you face to face, not through the printed word. So that's what we're going to do as we work through this book. We'll be talking. Together, we'll develop the guidelines that will work for you, in your field, at your stage in your career.

So join me now in a conversation about leadership for the future.

"*Until you risk everything, until you get to that point in life where you face losing everything — and overcome the fear — you're never going to lead.*"

- Dr. Tom Haggai
Chairman, IGA

LEADING TO THE 21ST CENTURY: ARE YOU LISTENING?

When Charlie Hunter came home from college in 1940, he brought something besides a college degree to help him out in the family business.

Hunter came equipped with a keen sense of hearing.

Back in those days, the Hunter family's 19-year-old dairy company was one of about 50 mom-and-pop dairies operating in the Piedmont area of the Carolinas.

Most of us who have been around long enough remember those chilled glass bottles of milk that waited on the front porch several mornings a week. We brought them in, along with the morning paper, and served the milk up with the news and a bowl of corn flakes.

That's the way about 90 percent of the milk in America reached the breakfast table.

But Charlie Hunter wasn't satisfied with the status quo. Hunter heard change in the wind. He listened to what it was saying. And he made it work for him.

Today, more than 50 years after Hunter brought home a sharp pair of ears tuned to change, Hunter Jersey Farms stands alone. It's the only one of those 50 small dairies still operating in this area. Because Charlie Hunter did more than respond to change when it came his way. He heard it coming and faced it head-on.

Hunter Dairy switched from glass bottles to paper cartons in 1947 — the first home-service dairy in the country to make that change. Only problem with that, Hunter was told by people in the industry nationwide, is that you're five years ahead of the times.

"We went ahead and made the plunge," Hunter said. "We weathered it. It was pretty rough financially, but I saw that I had to change and start selling milk the way people wanted to buy it."

With that experience under his belt, Hunter made a habit of staying one step ahead of change.

He anticipated the push for purification through pasteurization. He anticipated the effect major supermarket chains would have on his ability to make a profit on his product. He foresaw Americans' taste for convenience.

Hunter Jersey Farms is alive — and thriving — because Charlie Hunter saw change as an opportunity, and not something to fear.

Hunter's story is a lesson for every sales professional and manager who wants to lead.

Victims of Bad Hearing

Unfortunately, not everybody in business has Charlie Hunter's sharp hearing — or his willingness to take the plunge. Lots of folks in the business community seem to have a bad case of hearing loss when it comes to hearing the changes in the wind.

In more than 20 years of training for companies

throughout the U.S. and the world, I've had the chance to watch how business people have coped with the tremendous changes of the last two decades.

Some coped by listening and learning. Others tried to cope by holding fast to the ideas that helped them capture success in the first place. The history of business is filled with stories of people who weren't listening when the winds of change started whistling around board rooms and factories.

In the early 1970s, the Big Three auto makers in the U.S. weren't paying attention.

You know how that story turned out. While foreign auto makers were gauging which way the wind was blowing and responding with ever smaller, ever more efficient cars for the fuel- conscious consumer, GM, Ford and Chrysler kept rolling V-8 gas-guzzlers off the assembly lines.

Result: Japan and Germany ruled the world market for years. On a more sweeping scale, the same thing happened in the People's Republic of China in May of 1989.

For years, under the leadership of Deng Xiaoping, success through enterprise had been encouraged. Notions foreign to communist and socialist ideology seeped in slowly, almost silently. Farmers who produced more were rewarded with more money. Acquisition of personal property was permitted — and applauded. And young people were no longer discouraged from — or persecuted for — flaunting designer jeans from the West and dancing to the beat of music from the West.

But as loyalty to socialism irrevocably and showily eroded in the face of a growing passion for democracy and the entrepreneurial spirit, Deng Xiaoping wasn't paying attention.

The history books won't forget the struggle that raged in Tiananmen Square in May of 1989.

Thousands died because no one was listening to the unmistakable sounds of coming change.

That's much more tragic, of course, than a business closing its doors. But in a world where private enterprise and personal success are at the root of our society's success, do you want to be guilty of not keeping your ear to the ground?

The classic case is the railroad industry. With its big, iron monsters and tens of thousands of miles of track criss- crossing the country, the industry felt secure in its dominance. When people wanted to go, they booked a berth. When freight needed shipping, the steam engines rolled out.

The leaders of the railroads thought they were in the railroad business. They weren't. You and I know they were in the transportation industry.

And because they weren't listening when airplanes took to the skies and interstate highways brought the east coast closer to the west coast, they let a near monopoly in long-distance transportation dwindle to nothing.

Think about the communications industry. Which was once, at least in Western Union's thinking, the telegraph industry. Which became, in AT&T's mind, the long-distance telephone industry. Or, for the folks at the U.S. Postal Service and UPS, the overnight mail industry.

Which many people feel is now giving way to the fax industry.

The real point is, they were all talking about the communication industry.

An industry marked by change.

No Time to Adjust

As I researched this book by interviewing some of this nation's best leaders — in business, in public service, in sales, in athletics — what I found was almost unanimous agreement on one simple idea.

Almost to a person, the leaders I interviewed agreed that the most profound change in the business community during the next decade would be just that — change.

Change. It once happened over decades. It once came upon us gradually, gave us time to adjust, to rearrange our thinking. In those days, you landed a job at the age of 20 and could be pretty certain the same company would be giving you a gold watch at your retirement 45 years later.

Over those four decades, there was change. But it was so gradual, it didn't shake us up much.

Today, if you don't let change shake you up, you'd better be willing to go belly-up in whatever business you're in.

Early in my career, you could take a couple of years to make up your mind about career decisions, about new directions for your business.

I thought for years I was going to be a lawyer and spend my life in courtrooms. But, at the age of 15, I chanced into a part-time job on a local radio station. Something about sitting in that tiny room, wearing a headset that invariably didn't fit right, talking to nameless, faceless, voiceless people, beckoned to me.

I was astonished to find out an adult could make a living at something I enjoyed so much — so much I would have paid for the chance to do it.

But as I became successful locally, first at a Chapel Hill station during my college years and later at Charlotte's

WBT and WBTV, one of the nation's oldest and most respected AM radio and TV stations, I realized that people in radio and TV didn't have much control over their careers. Every 13 weeks, a new ratings book comes along and you might no longer be a valuable property.

I learned early the power of change.

I decided I wanted more control than that over my career, so I made up my mind to move into a new career. But I had years to make the change. I spent about five years edging from my radio and TV career into public speaking. I nursed both careers along until I could make the transition and earn a living as a speaker. I am forever grateful to my friend and leader Jim Babb, former President of Jefferson-Pilot Communications, for encouraging my growth and supporting my decision — he demonstrated first-hand some of the leadership qualities we'll talk about later.

Today, we don't have the luxury of debating our changes that long.

So the biggest change leaders must adjust to is the rapidity of change, the unrelentingly brisk change that barely allows us to catch our breath before it slips in something new again.

Unlimited Opportunity

We all know about the dramatic changes in the information industry. But one of the best examples of how to handle change, how to turn it to your advantage, comes from that stanchion of the status quo, the banking industry.

Hugh McColl proved his ability to react to change

when his NCNB Corporation grew to be the seventh largest U.S. bank. And he did it, not in spite of change, but by taking advantage of change. McColl saw, in the deregulation of the banking industry in the early 1980s, unlimited opportunity.

When deregulation legislation made it possible to serve contiguous states early in the last decade, McColl and a cadre of business partners jumped state lines into Florida while other banks were still debating — and debating and debating — how deregulation would affect them.

While everyone else was thinking about doing something, McColl and his partners were doing something.

That same kind of decisive action made McColl's efforts to expand successful. When First Republic Bank of Texas, the second-largest bank in the state, folded, McColl's NCNB Corporation bid for the bank's assets. He was competing against the likes of California's Wells Fargo, which is said to have sent in three of its people to await the FDIC's decision.

McColl wanted to be ready for the change if the decision fell in his direction, so he sent people, too.

Not three people; 250 people. He sent NCNB bank officials for every branch. He had printed materials ready. They had an entire company of NCNB's top executives there to reassure the customers of First Republic that their deposits were safe. And to reassure the employees that they were the bank's most precious asset. That they would see a continuum of good leadership.

That bank is now the seventh largest bank in America. That's what can happen when you know how to handle change. McColl is one of many who feel that the business leaders of the '90s and beyond must learn to cope with change. "Increased competition will put enormous pressures on management to change, be flexible, to turn on a dime," he said.

And most of us in the large companies that have dominated the business world of the '80s aren't equipped to handle that kind of rapid-fire, can't-catch-your-breath change. Like huge ocean liners, we change directions only slowly. But we would do well to note how quickly and sharply a 25-footer can negotiate a turn in the water. There's a huge lesson there.

Allan Hurst, who's made quite a name for himself as a sales and management consultant, pointed out, "Big business gets all the press for screaming and yelling about how they're being strangled by Washington. The small business owner says nothing and just adjusts.

"You can bet five days after a bill is signed in Washington, the small business owner already has a strategy to counteract it."

Big business, on the other hand, spends too much time and too many dollars trying to figure out how to react — like many of McColl's competitors in banking.

Rising to the Challenge

Jeff Mullins, who has lead his UNC-Charlotte basketball team to national prominence, feels too many of us have fallen victim to an old philosophy that lets us hold onto the comfortable status quo.

"On the collegiate level, too many presidents and chancellors put their heads in the sand and get too far removed. Until there is a problem, they don't want to talk about it," Mullins said. "If it's not broken, don't fix it —

when they haven't looked to see if maybe it's breaking and corroding."

Dr. Tom Haggai, chairman of IGA, also rejects the old "if it's not broke..." axiom.

"We must lead people to understand that life is a series of interruptions," he said. "We can't be hassled or intimidated by events because we expect it and are challenged to rise above the status quo.

"Leadership should be skeptical of the sacrosanct, should believe things should be examined, should constantly try to improve any given circumstance."

So we must learn from the people who react by acting. We have to learn to make decisions quickly, to find ways to put those decisions into operation tomorrow and not at the beginning of the next fiscal year.

Reacting to change with flexibility instead of inertia results in more than business growth, more than increased sales. The risk-taking that goes along with riding the crest of change, according to Dr. Haggai, becomes a trial by fire for leaders.

"Until you risk everything, until you get to that point in life where you face losing everything — and overcome the fear — you're never going to lead," he said.

So it is more than willingness to change that sets the true leaders apart. It is seeking out change and wringing every bit of potential out of it that takes you to the next horizon in your own growth.

Remember Charlie Hunter. Clearly, leaders are risk-takers. If you aren't pushing the limits, if you aren't making decisions that keep even your staunchest supporters wondering if you've gone too far this time, then you may not have what it takes to lead into the 21st Century.

Battling Inertia

As tough as it is to set ourselves up for that kind of risk- taking, what is even harder is persuading others to make change.

"One of our biggest obstacles in dealing with people," McColl said, "is inertia. People resist change. So one of the most difficult things to get people to do is to change their behavior — even if it's in their best interest."

Dr. Jim Tunney, a former school official who now serves as one of the NFL's top referees, agrees.

"Change threatens people because it threatens their power," said Tunney. "It threatens their security, it threatens their adjustment. We're going to have to help people understand that change and risk are part of their business."

It's part of our business. As surely as delivering a quality product or meeting a deadline or preparing a sales presentation that shows we're savvy with computer graphics, adapting to change and willingness to run risks are requisites for tomorrow's high-achievers. As leaders, we have to prepare ourselves and our people for that.

And this means, more than anything else, keeping our co-workers, our team, with us as we head toward change.

Team-building for Tomorrow

"Most of us are hesitant to change the way we do things and leaders are typically trying to push in new directions, so there is an inherent conflict," said John Fox, president of Bostik. "To get people to move in those new directions, you have to overcome the natural inclination to stay on familiar turf. That requires someone who can inspire and motivate, perhaps cajole or push."

We'll talk in depth about team-building for the decade and the century ahead — what I like to think of as business bonding — in Chapter Three.

But briefly, we do it through communication. We do it by making the challenges fun, by enjoying the process of exploring alternatives and looking for new answers. We do it by encouraging, expecting, demanding innovation. We do it by allowing our people to be a valued, respected part of the process.

We do it by accepting that risk makes some failure inevitable. In others. In ourselves.

I want to talk more about our attitudes on failure later. But the gist of what most true leaders will tell you is that we must change our attitude about failure.

We can't allow ourselves — or others — to translate failure into personal defeat.

So my toughest challenge to you, if you want to be one of the change-agents in your company's future, is to be — not just willing to face change. But eager to seek it out. "Fire-in-the-belly" hungry for it. And then so enthusiastic about it that you have to make little effort to persuade others — they will be persuaded by your very enthusiasm.

Hungry for Change

Let's look again, briefly, at a few of the ways we infect others with our enthusiasm for change.

1. Face change head-on and quickly.
2. Court change. Anticipate it by remaining a life long student of your profession, by keeping your eye

on fields that touch the edges of your profession.

3. Encourage your workers to court change by rewarding innovation, by giving them all freedom to dream.

4. See failure as an opportunity learned from, not an opportunity missed.

What are some of the changes we must be prepared to face? As you might imagine, they change every day. And will change even more rapidly as the future is upon us. But some of the major ones, mentioned time and again by the leaders I've interviewed, are:

- The changing workforce
- Making a personal contribution
- A concrete commitment to quality, value and service
- The global economy

I'll deal with each of these in detail, exposing you to the best ideas of the best leaders this nation has to offer. But each of these ideas, every technique we discuss, every theory I ask you to buy into as we prepare ourselves for the 21st Century, will be molded by a common theme. A recurring idea that must become the cornerstone of all that American business is trying to build as we head for the year 2000.

A return to ethics. The cry for a return to ethics, to the values upon which this nation relied for so long, echoed resoundingly as I made my rounds interviewing leaders. If we ignore this cry, if we think we can continue to heap success upon success without regard for values and ethics, we are playing ostrich much more dangerously even than the auto makers in the early '70s, who really believed that Americans would soon abandon their love affair with the small car.

Let's move on, and get our heads out of the sand.

Next: The Number One Challenge Facing Leadership

"When you look at the Ten Commandments, they were not the Ten Suggestions. There are certain basic values that we need to live by. And if we don't live by those basic values, we're going to do ourselves in. Empires throughout history have ruined themselves mostly through corruptness."

- Dr. Jim Tunney
NFL Referee

SPREADING AMERICA'S ETHICS EPIDEMIC

2

Major General William Dean was a condemned man. His North Korean captors told him he would be executed unless he revealed certain military secrets.

For Major General Dean, the choice was simple: He must prepare for his execution.

The most important part of his preparation for what seemed to be the inevitable was a letter to his young son, Bill. He wanted to leave behind something to help the youngster, to guide him over the hurdles life would throw in his path. Hurdles that Bill would have to face without a father's helping hand.

The letter Dean wrote gave young Bill one word to remember, one word to guide him past any roadblocks life had to offer.

The word was integrity. It's what you look for in an elected official, Dean wrote.

It's what you look for in your dentist, your minister, your mate for life, your fellow worker. I may not be there for you, Dean wrote to Bill, but if you choose integrity you will have chosen the high road.

Things have changed since 1953, when the North Koreans finally released Major General Dean, who had chosen the high road for all the months of his captivity.

You don't need me to tell you how much things have changed. Evidence of that change greets us in the morning paper and on the evening news every day. The HUD scandals. The shame of Leona Helmsley. The fall of politicians and men of the cloth, and athletes who can no longer be heroes, and people in public service who decided to serve themselves first, the public last.

For the last 40 years in America, the high road has been the road less traveled.

I'm not sure how or why it happened. Some say it grows out of our business history, which gives our leaders some paternalistic power over our lives. A power which seemed to say that the boss man has all the answers, is always right and therefore owes no allegiance to the rules the rest of us must follow.

Others suggest the decline in integrity is the result of the cynicism that grew out of the disappointed idealism of the '60s, when our nation came face to face with the harsh realities of assassinations and political cover-ups and death on foreign shores.

Or maybe it's just plain greed, as others suggest. I'm not sure why. And I'm not sure it matters why. What does matter is that it cannot continue. That is the call to arms I've heard loud and clear from some of this nation's greatest leaders.

Cheating Your Way to the Top

"The integrity factor — the problem of straight out not

being honest — has hurt American business, the whole entity of the United States, in the past decade," said NFL referee Dr. Jim Tunney. "That has to change. We cannot continue on a road of doing whatever we think we can get away with.

"We don't have to do business by cheating."

Without being prompted, without hearing from me that others had hit on the same sore spot, most of the leaders I interviewed spoke passionately about the return to ethics which is necessary if American business is to recapture its position of leadership in the world.

They spoke of it as the number one challenge facing America today. They spoke of it with passion and dismay and humility. And they spoke of it as if it were their personal responsibility to begin the march back up the high road.

And they are right. Our return to ethics will have to be lead by people like you. People who are leading us to greater profit margins and innovative growth will also be the ones to lead us back to a time of renewed faith in the principles of integrity so vividly demonstrated by Major General Dean.

"The challenge for today's leader is not so much the knowledge of the product or the knowledge of the company, but the ability to lead with integrity," said another sports figure, former Miami University basketball coach Bill Foster. "And we've got to hope it filters down. Because if it doesn't, we're all in trouble. This integrity challenge is in a category by itself. Whatever comes second is a distant second."

Foster throws down a tremendous challenge to American business leaders. It is a challenge we must be prepared to meet. Because America and the world will not continue to overlook the lack of ethics that mars the way we do business.

Demanding Integrity

I'd like to take Foster's challenge one step farther. We've got to do more than hope it will filter down. We've got to use our role as leaders to make sure it filters down.

How many times have you heard it? The most significant, the most effective way for leaders to lead is — that's right — by example.

We lead by example. So in this case, what I'm urging you to do is step into the forefront of an ethics epidemic in American business. Show others by your example that you have chosen Dean's high road. That you demand integrity of yourself and that you demand it of those around you.

Let others learn by watching you that all your business decisions are ruled by certain values. Values that are inviolable. Values that are as crucial to your success as meeting your quotas and making your deadlines and closing another big sale.

Jim Jensen at 3-M has been setting that kind of example for years.

"I am extremely hung up on honesty," Jensen said. "I tell every new person that works for me that this is a personal hang-up. I just cannot tolerate dishonesty and they ought to be aware of that right up front."

Sad to say, but that kind of straightforwardness is so rare that some folks in business just don't know how to handle it. I remember reading in Life magazine about

Jane Pauley's departure from "Good Morning, America." The story recounted how Pauley recognized that change was in the wind. Instead of waiting for those changes to take her by surprise, she decided to chart her own changing path.

She went to NBC execs and said that, since they had a new team in place, she wanted to take the opportunity to spend more time with her children. She would retire, without pay. The NBC execs, according to the Life story, were flabbergasted. They wondered what she was angling for.

The story reads: "'They were terribly confused,' an executive who deals with NBC explains with a chuckle, 'because she was telling them the truth and they had no experience with people who tell the truth.'"

Humorous reading, but sad commentary, wouldn't you agree?

RX for the Ethics Epidemic

So what I propose to you is this: As part of your personal long-range plan, vow to become a part of the ethics epidemic.

I'm not just talking about ethics with a capital "E," either. I'm not just talking about making sure you keep your hands clean when it comes to something that's going to land you in front of a grand jury. I'm talking about more than embezzlement and fraud and the kind of muscle-flexing tactics we only associate with the big boys who play real-life Monopoly with wads of million-dollar bills.

I'm talking about those things, too. That goes without

saying. But I'm also talking about personal accountability on a very individual, on a very small scale.

Art Linkletter, TV personality and business person, came along in the shadow of old-fashioned ethics. He points out that every little thing we do is part of the example we set for those who follow our lead.

"You have to be a role model in that you don't make any shortcuts or show your troops that you don't indulge in cheating on expense accounts or travel expenses," Linkletter said. "Because the person at the top can affect the entire organization. Once the word gets out that the person at the top is shallow or cheap or unethical, the organization is gone."

Good people will either leave, he concluded, or begin to do things the way the person at the top does things.

What does this mean for you? It means you can make a difference. Integrity starts with the individual. You can help mold the ethical atmosphere of your entire office, your entire department, your entire organization, with your own decision to follow a set of values in which you believe. It can start with you.

"Internal corruptness does not start with the government. It does not start with somebody else," Tunney said. "It starts with the individual. Which says to me: These are things I shouldn't do. These are things I've got to believe in, values I'm not going to violate."

Management trainer Don Thoren also points out that the simple fact of being accused of impropriety these days can have a lasting effect.

"Today, people truly believe that where there's smoke, there's fire," Thoren said. "In spite of our legal philosophy that says people are innocent until proven guilty, that's really not true among leaders in organizations today.

"Once challenged, they are tainted with the appearance of impropriety...in a way that makes it almost impossible for them ever to free themselves of that image."

A former basketball coach who faced the consequences of America's stepped-up scrutiny when the NCAA cited his team for a number of infractions came out of his downfall with a heightened sense of his own responsibility.

"Accountability is a tremendous watchword today, whatever business you're in," he said. "At one point, the concept that 'I wasn't aware of that' was perhaps an okay defense. If someone else was doing something they ought not to do, as long as you didn't have any knowledge of it, somehow it freed you of any blame, any culpability.

"I think what we're seeing today is a very high personal standard that we're going to hold our leaders to. A standard far above everyone, if they're going to be in that position of leadership. We're expecting our leaders to have a higher degree of integrity, a higher degree of ethics, a higher moral code and to accept a higher level of accountability for the entire operation."

The field of athletics, no doubt because of the constant spotlight under which it operates, has become aware of this growing demand for ethics and accountability before some of us in the business world. Like Tunney and Foster, Coach Jeff Mullins sees a pressing need to reaffirm our values.

And he feels the pressure comes from more than public opinion. The values are a vital part of the foundation on which we build our success, Mullins believes.

"Obviously, people like Boesky on Wall Street had the passion and the drive necessary to meet his goals," Mullins said. "But the integrity was missing. You don't have to do it with integrity, but I tend to think it crumbles sooner or later if you don't."

Carving Your Own Tablets

How do we put integrity back into the board room? Where do we start? Where do we find the guidelines?

Wally Amos, the magnate who brings out the kid in all of us with his Famous Amos Chocolate Chip Cookies, believes it starts with concept we all understand — the mission statement.

"It seems most people think our mission is just to make money," Amos said. "They'll do whatever it takes to make as much money as possible. So maybe we need to redefine our mission, our collective mission. And then maybe everyone individually needs to create their own mission statement. What is your personal mission for being here?"

He's right on target. We have to set up the guidelines, just as we set up the guidelines for hiring new people or evaluating employees. That way, the ethics that guide our professional actions aren't fuzzy. They aren't subject to re-interpretation for convenience's sake.

We've got to carve some tablets.

First, let me acknowledge that I am not the one to be suggesting what your values need to be. I am not the one to define integrity for American business in general or you in particular. You were hoping I'd make it easy, weren't you? The Ten Commandments According to Boyd.

I'm here to tell you: It ain't that easy.

Since confronting this issue at the prompting of some

of this nation's most respected leaders, I've grappled almost daily with what that code of ethics ought to be. And I've decided no one individual could — or even should — lay down the law for governing the ethics of another individual.

So what I lay at your feet is the problem of developing your own code. For yourself as an individual. For your company, perhaps. For the department for which you're responsible. For your family. You must decide how far your values will extend.

But I'm not going to abandon you entirely. In listening to my colleagues, in struggling with my own fuzzily-defined value system, I've come up with the following guidelines to govern your trip to the mountain. Whatever you carve on the tablets may be uniquely yours. But whatever those commandments end up including, let your decisions be guided by these thoughts.

• *Stop short-term thinking.* My old friend Linkletter has a hunch that this is one of the jumping off points for the whole problem, and he may be right. Short-term thinking, in business, is today's bottom-line thinking. We aren't concerned with where today's decisions will leave us in ten years, but with making the profit today.

"Greed. That short-term thinking is one of the worst traits I see in American business leaders today," said Dr. Haggai, echoing Linkletter's thoughts.

"This preoccupation with material gain leads to unethical practices and a greedy cannibalism of other countries," Linkletter said. "Unfortunately, we have equated success with money for so long that the success/failure perception of a person depends upon how much money he makes. That's a basic flaw in a system driven by greed."

A solution, which Linkletter suggests, leads to our next guideline:

• *Retool your definition of success.* Look for other ways to measure your own success and the success of others. The bottom-line, the bank account, the credit card limit don't necessarily reflect true value.

And that's the new criteria we've got to add to our measuring stick: Values.

Harvey Gantt, an architect and public servant, recently made national headlines with his challenge to a U.S. Senate veteran of 18 years. And he feels that today's young people have already beat us to realizing the significance of a strong value system.

"You see youngsters talking about going into careers again that don't necessarily pay the biggest bucks," said Gantt. "I've got two daughters who are talking about being doctors. Not just your everyday doctor with an office who sees middle-class patients. They want to go into under-served areas of the world.

"You know, that's a good sign." He's right. It is a good sign that the next generation may already have discovered that values have to figure into our definition of success.

Linkletter cited a wonderful example of just how warped our judgments of success can become if we eliminate that element of values.

"Adolph Hitler was one of the most successful men in history for 15 years," he pointed out. "He did everything well that he wanted to do: kill Jews, conquer people, disrupt the world."

But, he went on to add, if you plug in values — and not simply money or power or short-term gain — Hitler's success quotient is suddenly on very shaky ground.

• *Reject the conspiracy of silence.* This unofficial conspiracy is at the heart of many of our business dealings and is one of the reasons that lack of integrity has been able to gain such a foothold in American business.

You know what I mean. You have lunch once a week with the members of your civic club. They're your friends, your fellow movers and shakers, the people who make up the foundation of your community's economy. So you break bread together, swap jokes, share information, lend support.

Yet, the man who always sits at the head of the table runs a company that is polluting a major river in your state. The woman at your left uses her position to sway political decisions that will affect the dollar value of her personal property. The man who reads the minutes is a well-known advocate for a private club that refuses membership to Blacks and Jews.

And what do you do about it? Nothing. "You don't read too many articles about the top CEOs of major companies standing up and saying XYZ Corporation is polluting and that's irresponsible," said Hugh McColl. "Business leaders have remained silent about the excesses of other business leaders. Even when they disapprove and think it's wrong, on issues where it's clear that a thinking person would disagree with what's being done. Yet they don't speak out.

"That's a failure of American business." Bucking that conspiracy of silence, however, takes an awful lot of good, old-fashioned guts. And perhaps not a small measure of foolhardiness. You know how it is when you single yourself out and decide to swim against the tide. You become a target for ridicule. Or worse, retaliation.

Remember Jimmy Stewart in that classic Frank Capra film, "Mr. Smith Goes to Washington"? A real innocent to the ways of the world, Stewart's character ended up as a member of Congress, where he was expected to play by the old "you scratch my back and I'll scratch yours" rules. When he discovered that such back- scratching extended to breaking what he saw as the real rules — the rules of integrity and fair-play and decency — he refused to join in the game.

Even if you've never seen the film, you can easily imagine what happened. The political machine that Stewart's character tried to expose turned the tables and painted a picture of corruption with Stewart's character at its center. Before the movie ended, he'd been disgraced and humiliated and degraded.

"Mr. Smith Goes to Washington" has, as Hollywood so often manages, a happy ending. Truth was vindicated and Jimmy Stewart got the girl.

But if you decide to break the conspiracy of silence, you must be prepared for the fact that Frank Capra won't be directing.

You must be prepared for the fact that you can, if you aren't judicious, end up an outcast with few colleagues on your side.

Are there ways to break the conspiracy without ending up with yourself cast as the villain? There are. You'll no doubt think of some yourself — and I hope you'll share them with me. But to get you started thinking, a few of the cautions you may want to take are to:

1. Make your first conversation a face-to-face one with the person whose stand you question. Clear the air. State your case clearly, without rancor, without finger-pointing. Ask this colleague's help in finding solutions. See if you can make this person a part of the solution. Seek his or her involvement in a community task force to address the problem. Suggest working side-by-side to educate the community, to raise funds, to put a plan in place.

2. **Never let the differences become personal.** If your colleague refuses to become a part of the solution, make sure your intentions are clear. You plan to fight the problem. But you don't intend to fight a personal battle. Then, stick to your intentions. If at all possible, don't call names. Don't discuss anything about your colleague or his/her company except the issue at stake. Don't answer personal charges your colleague may subsequently make about you. Stick to the issue.

3. **Do your homework.** Don't stick your nose into the issue in the first place unless you're well-educated about it. Know what you're talking about, so you don't run the risk of taking a stance that may turn out to be the wrong stance. Talk to experts — and not just on the side you support. Read. Research. Give yourself a firm grounding in the facts. Finding out the facts — all the facts — can sometimes be a tremendous eye-opener.

4. **Wage your war, as much as possible, behind the scenes.** That doesn't, however, mean behind anybody's back. It means away from the glare of a TV camera, without the help of the local newspaper. It means not on the lectern at the Rotary meeting, in front of everyone else who'll then begin to wonder when you'll turn on them. It means through personal contacts, through individual persuasion. Be up front, but try not to make the front page.

5. **Be prepared for the backlash.** You may lose

business friends. And you know what that means. You may lose customers. You may make enemies out of people who've been on your family's Christmas card list for decades.

But if you are sincere and above-board and if you choose your battles carefully, you may find supporters who are grateful that someone has finally broken the conspiracy of silence.

One of the best ways you can avoid losing friends once you decide to champion your beliefs? By all means:

6. Avoid sanctimony. Need I say more?

The easiest course is certainly silence. You need strength if you decide not to take the easy course, that is certain.

But Major General Dean never promised Bill that choosing the high road would be easy.

• *Establish a strong spiritual base for yourself.* Your base may be different from mine. It may not rely upon a weekly visit to church or synagogue. But acknowledging the part of yourself that is a part of some greater whole, that is in tune with some universal scheme, will give you strength. And that, in turn, will make it somewhat easier to choose the high road.

• *Establish a code of ethics for your company.* You don't have to do it alone. In fact, it's better if you don't. Turn it into a team-building exercise. Get everyone involved. Find out what values, what standards they would like to bring into the daily operation of your organization, your department. Spend a day in retreat, hashing out ideas. Synthesize those ideas, let them simmer, then bring the group back together to reach final consensus.

"We have our business ethics written out and shared

with everybody, passed down through the organization," said 3-M's Jim Jensen. "Our CEO, at least twice a year when he has our executive conference group together, hits that as very important. He talks about why it's important from a business standpoint as well as from a personal standpoint.

"It's very simple. We will never knowingly violate the letter or spirit of the law in any place where we do business."

Wouldn't it be great if it were that simple in every business?

• *Remember that perception is reality.* Sounds like double-talk, I know. But what I mean is very simply this: If people believe that something is true, if it has every appearance in the general public's mind of being true, it might as well be true. People will accept it as true. And once that perception is established in people's minds, it is almost impossible to change that perception.

That principle will work against us if the finger is ever pointed, as Thoren pointed out. Once accused, we'll have a hard time changing the minds of the public.

What you and I need to learn from that is how important it is to do nothing to create a perception that we are in some way lacking in integrity. Because perceptions, as you can see, linger. And are hard to erase.

"It's important in running your business that you be — not just honest with what you're doing — but you've got to be above suspicion," Tunney said. "We have to create in people the feeling that we're so doggone honest that we'd never do something dishonest. That's the kind of direction American business has to go."

• *Admit your mistakes.* It doesn't get much simpler than that. We all make them. We might as well admit it. It does wonders for your credibility and your conscience.

• *Establish a code that allows for the other person's opinions and beliefs.* You may be a vegetarian, but that doesn't make it smart — or acceptable — to picket the restaurant of a colleague because he serves a nine-ounce filet. Being dogmatic is not a good substitute for championing your beliefs.

When your decisions infringe on the rights of someone else, it's time to take a long, hard look at what you're doing.

• *Ask yourself, as you make your decisions — personal or business — if you will be glad for your grandchildren to live with the consequences of your decisions.* If you can't satisfy yourself that tomorrow's generations won't suffer from what you're doing, maybe you need to do a little soul-searching.

• *Don't hang yourself up seeking a model of perfection, in yourself or in your colleagues.* Let's be realistic for a moment. Perfection isn't within our grasp and, in many respects, may not be what we want for ourselves anyway.

Down through the ages, some of the people who have been most effective in re-routing the energies of a group have been excessive people, people who were anything but balanced models of perfection.

Two of my heroes, John Kennedy and Martin Luther King, demonstrated incomparable integrity in the areas where they exercised leadership, yet were weak if measured in other areas.

Adam Clayton Powell, a man who first galvanized this nation's Blacks with his leadership decades ago, was known for his excesses. Richard Nixon, who opened the doors that separated the West from Red China, was found seriously lacking.

Howard Hughes was a singular leader in both the film and the air transportation industries during their infancies; his successes transcended the phobias that ruled his life in later years.

The tough question to answer is when do our personal imperfections begin to color our professional lives?

Putting Values to Work

I hope I've given you enough food for thought to get you started on your search for your own personal code of ethics. But to keep you thinking in that vein, what I want to do now is talk about some specific ways that our values and standards can affect the kind of leader we are. The kind of leader we will need to become for the years ahead.

In future chapters, we'll talk about applying your values to a number of the issues you'll have to face as a leader:

- Team-building for the future
- Managing your power
- Facing your failures
- Giving back to the community
- Rediscovering quality and service

The struggle with our ethics will be with us always. Deciding what code governs our ethics won't make it much easier, but it will help.

What will help most of all is deciding that we're all going to pull together in the ethics epidemic that must sweep this nation if we are to remain at the top.

Next: Business Bonding

"We never worried about willing cooperation at one time — we couldn't have cared less...Nowadays, if you tell somebody, 'Do it my way or else,' they may take the 'or else.'"

- John Ralston
NFL coach

BUSINESS BONDING: TEAM-BUILDING FOR TOMORROW

3

Tom Carpenter's first taste of leadership was in Officer's Candidate School at Ft. Benning, Ga.

Every young infantry officer there wore an arm patch on his left shoulder that read, "Follow me."

"The idea in the Army is that if the second lieutenant says 'let's go,' people don't have time to stand around and have a conference about it," said Carpenter, a senior executive with Aetna Life and Casualty. "If they do, they're going to get killed. So they teach the young soldiers to have complete confidence in their leader and when the leader decides what the group is going to do, everyone is instantly on board."

Wouldn't it be nice if it were that easy outside OCS? But we all know it isn't. When we're hired for the job, no one slaps a "Follow me" patch on our shoulder. When we're assigned to the mission, we know our people won't have blind faith in what we do — and when you come right down to it, aren't you glad of that?

"When a follower is a blind sheep, I don't think that indicates a very good leader," said Dot Ridings, a Knight-

Ridder Publishing executive. "I want followers who are committed, rather than people doing something because I say so."

So if you're going to be a leader — in sales, in service, in production, whatever — your first step is to find yourself a team. To earn yourself a following.

And, no disrespect intended, in the business world of tomorrow, you won't do that the way they've done it at Ft. Benning and Parris Island in recent decades. You don't do it by barking orders and issuing commands and forcing loyalty through intimidation.

Coaching the Mental

But you've got to find a way to do it. Jim Tunney, whose years with the NFL have given him a unique vantage point on competition and team-building, said this about team-building for the future: "The competition is becoming so strong that the strongest team, the people who work closest together, who believe in each other, who will follow the direction of the leader and the vision of the leader, those teams will last longer than the ones who are just trying to band-aid the problem."

Tunney dropped a lot of clues to the process as he goes about defending the importance of the team. He talked about working closely together and believing in each other. Phrases that reinforce Coach John Ralston's assertion that coaching — one of the most visible forms of team-building in America today — has changed dramatically.

"We used to coach the team, but we don't any more — we coach individuals," said Ralston, who has coached football at Stanford University, as well as for the NFL's

Denver Broncos and the San Francisco 49ers. "We used to coach the physical, now we coach the mental.

"We never worried about willing cooperation at one time — we couldn't have cared less. You wear your hair a certain way, you dress a certain way and, if you want to be a member of the team, you do it this way. Nowadays, if you tell somebody, 'Do it my way or else,' they may take the 'or else.'"

What's the message there? "Follow me" in today's world isn't an order. It had better be a process of persuasion.

Today's team-building is a bonding process. It's built on trust and confidence and a knowledge that reaching the goal is a victory for everyone.

It's a two-part proposition, really. Part attitude and part action.

Attitude. Action. I'm going to take them one at a time. And I'm going to talk about the more important of the two first, and save the other for Chapter Four.

I'm going to talk about attitude. Because if you don't get attitude right, chances are slim that any of your actions will make a difference.

Let's break attitude down into four specific areas, then discuss them one at a time.

1. Can Do vs. No Way
2. A caring attitude
3. Challenging your co-workers
4. Fire in the belly

Can Do vs. No Way

Kay Yow, women's basketball coach at North Carolina State University, said there is one leadership trait over which we have 100 percent control: Attitude.

And, although we're devoting the rest of this chapter to different aspects of attitude, let's talk first about the tone of our attitude. Are we optimists or pessimists? Are we enthusiasts or complainers? Is our reaction "Can do" or "No way"?

If you go after a job with a "can do" attitude, you're probably in the minority.

"Society tends to view things in a 'can't be done' mode," said another coach. "The pessimists have us out-numbered! You're going to find many more people to tell you why you can't get something done than those who say, 'that's a great idea.'"

Coach Bill Foster always taught his players that atti-tude determines altitude. "If you can just keep working every day to keep your attitude positive and upbeat, the sky's the limit. I have players who played for me 10 years ago and they'll send me a note with the Zig Ziglar phrase I always used at the bottom. 'Attitude determines alti-tude.'"

He couldn't be more right. So much of an organiza-tion's success, an individual's success is based, not on product knowledge or sales ability or management skills, but on attitude. Leaders must envision the high side. I'm not saying be a Pollyanna. But I am saying that you must recognize the importance of the atmosphere you create.

Because keep in mind, when people talk about whether a company is a good place to work, they're not talking about whether the thermostat is set too high or too low or whether there are enough pencils in the supply cabinet.

They're talking about an attitude. There's more power in changing attitude than in changing all the machinery in your plant. The Japanese beat the socks off us in so many ways when we had gleaming new equipment and they were using old, out-dated stuff.

A recent episode of CBS's "60 Minutes" profiled Herb Kelleher, CEO of Dallas-based Southwest Airlines. Southwest is an enormously successful airline that breaks all kinds of rules. One of the things Kelleher is known for is loyal and productive employees.

"It may sound like outright flackery except that Wall Street analysts say it's true," said CBS reporter Steve Kroft. "In a business where productivity equals profits, Southwest has the lowest turnover and the best labor relations in the industry...They do it out of pride, profit-sharing and because they like their boss."

The report went on to emphasize that Kelleher's enthusiasm spilled over to his employees, via such unusual vehicles as a company video complete with a rap song delivered by employees and an honors and recognition party staged annually, at which Kelleher is one of the liveliest partiers.

"I love our people, you know," Kelleher told "60 Minutes." "And it's very simple. I love them. They kid me, they make fun of me, they're irreverent towards me, they're a joy to be with. And I think there's a kind of reciprocal thing going on there. They know that I love them, that I respect them and that I'm proud of them."

If he can get that kind of coverage out of "60 Minutes," he must be doing plenty right!

Jim Tunney agrees that one of the biggest 'people' obstacles the leader faces is people who have been programmed to react negatively. Leaders must not only make sure they don't let the negativism creep into their own attitude. They must also fight their best battle to make sure their own positive attitude is victor in the battle of the attitudes.

"When you get a negative person to overcome one small obstacle, one small negative attitude and they can begin to see there's something to this positiveness, they begin to change," Tunney said.

Tunney remembers when he became principal of a high school and inherited a faculty of teachers who had let a negative attitude become the dominant trait of the group. What did he do?

"Rather than spend a lot of time working on changing their negative attitude, I spent my energy working with the people who were positive," Tunney said. "First it was a small circle, then it became a bigger circle. A sort of centrifugal force took over. And every time it circled around again, we would suck in one of these people who were in the negative circle and pretty soon most of the people were on board."

Read that over. The lesson is an important one. Fighting against something can be exhausting, can be discouraging, can be an element of negativism in and of itself. Don't fall into that trap.

Instead of fighting against something, use the flow of energy to your advantage. In this case, find the pocket of optimism and keep it moving forward.

How do you do that? By remembering that enthusiasm is caught, not taught, according to Coach Bill Foster and businessman Art Linkletter.

"Your enthusiasm is very infectious, very contagious," said Linkletter. "If your attitude is enthusiastic, friendly, curious, then you're getting the most from people as well as giving the most."

That's so important. You're getting the most from people. And the reason is simple. It's because you're giving the most of yourself.

What a positive approach to team-building. What a sure-fire way to put together a can't-lose group of co-workers.

Remember, if you can change attitudes, you can change the direction of a nation. Ghandi did it. Martin Luther King did it. Ronald Reagan did it. Nelson Mandella did it. Winston Churchill, too. So did Rosa Parks, in a city bus in Montgomery, Alabama, in the early 1960s.

And you can do it for your office. For your department. For your sales force. For your company.

A Caring Attitude

The best leaders are human beings first, bosses second. Each time I visit Southern Shows, Inc., I re-learn that simple but powerful tenet of leadership from the example Joan Zimmerman lives.

Zimmerman and her husband, Bob, started 30 years ago with a spring flower and garden show to compete with shows put on in the northeast. Today, their Southern Shows are responsible for more than a dozen and a half consumer and trade shows in eight southeastern cities, drawing more than half a million visitors each year. Southern Shows is the granddaddy of shows in this part of the country.

But each time she walks through her headquarters, Zimmerman reminds me that leaders are people, too.

And she does it by treating the 20-plus people in her company like human beings. Without blowing smoke, Zimmerman will introduce you to every person in her organization. And she will tell you several things that make each person outstanding. In a 15-minute sweep through her offices, she will have clearly made each person feel special.

She uses that personal touch to her advantage, too. Because she knows her people so well, because she stays in such close touch with everyone in her operation, she knows right away when Southern Shows isn't hitting on all cylinders.

"When I see that someone is developing unusual habits, like constantly being late or being out sick more than usual, I address it immediately," Zimmerman said. "I ask if something is wrong. Not if there is something wrong with you. But is there something wrong here that we need to do something about.

"We don't dabble in their personal affairs, but as it pertains to the business, we keep up with what's going on."

That kind of personal involvement impacts on productivity for the Zimmermans, not only because it helps them spot potential problems before they develop into real problems, but also because it reinforces the fact that the Zimmermans care.

Herb Kelleher, the airline CEO who came out looking like a prince on "60 Minutes," demonstrated that kind of caring for his people. And they rewarded him with loyalty, by being productive, by cheerfully delivering the kind of service that also wins loyalty from customers and clients.

Dale Brown, basketball coach at LSU, considers large doses of love sprinkled with discipline is true leadership.

"I learned it from Monseigneur John Hogan, one of my heroes, who was the coach and principal of my high school in Minot, N.D.," Brown said. "He was firm, yet in all his firmness, he always possessed love. Leadership is when you get into the people's lives. You don't have to hug a cow to get her in the right pasture. You can manage a herd of cows.

"But leadership is much more compassionate." One of the ways Brown tries to put that compassion to work is by remembering to relate as one human being to another. "I try to remember myself in that stage of life, at that player's age, and remember how it felt. We tend to have amnesia about our past the older we get. We forget the things we did, what it was like."

If Brown can use that technique with college-age athletes, is there any reason why we can't think to do it with the adults we lead — no matter what their age or their stage of development?

Brown suggests we assume the motto of the Salvation Army as one of our rules of leadership: To love those who aren't loved by anyone else.

"If we did that in leadership, we could clear up the criminal, racial and unemployment problems," Brown declared. "If we did that, I don't think the world would end because someone pushed a button."

I believe he's right. And if packing that kind of caring into our briefcase of leadership skills could have such an impact on the world, just imagine what it could do for your productivity, for your level of service, for your reputation for excellence.

Even, as a serendipitous by-product of all the rest, for your bottom line.

Challenging Your People

Jeff Mullins, who has lifted the basketball program at UNC-Charlotte to national prominence, believes most of us limit ourselves in some way.

He asked me to imagine that he and I went out to the local high school track for our afternoon jog and ran until we were both exhausted. Now he asked me to imagine that our biggest hero — Billy Graham, let's say, for the sake of conversation — stopped by the track and waved as we passed, dripping perspiration and limping in our Nikes.

"I believe we could dig deep and probably go 10 more laps simply because the leader we admire and want to impress showed up," Mullins said. "We all have a wall we run into in our minds before we've really run into it. We say we're going to run six laps and it's hard to run that seventh because we've put that six up there.

"True leaders take us beyond that wall and carry us through that wall where individually we couldn't make it."

Joan Zimmerman believes that need to challenge people is going to be one of the key issues each of us must face in leading through the final decade of the century.

"We're working with a better-educated, more demanding employee in many instances than ever before. The kind of people we're now dealing with are not just workers," she said. "Our biggest challenge is going to be keeping these associates challenged. I don't mean happy, I mean challenged."

Mae Douglas, Director of Human Resources for Ciba-Geigy Corporation, also urges leaders to remember that they're dealing with employees who are often smart and sophisticated — employees who need a challenge.

"People want to do more than just come to work and be told what to do," Douglas said. "If people feel they are making a contribution, that they have a say about their work, that inspires them to want to come to work every-day."

Trainer Don Thoren challenges us to learn how to challenge others by getting to know our people: their hopes and dreams and aspirations and beliefs.

"Leaders must truly understand these things if they're going to be successful in helping people channel their energies toward the pursuit of a worthy goal," Thoren said.

In Chapter Four, Thoren has some outstanding advice on how to learn what motivates people.

The first step to challenging is understanding. As the people who populate our workplace have changed, so have the incentives that pump them up. Once upon a time, money would do it. Once upon a time, a Christmas turkey might help. Today, we have to remember John Ralston's advice: We're coaching individuals, not teams.

"The essence of leadership is in correctly ascertaining and responding to the needs of the people you're leading," said Jim Heavner, CEO for The Village Companies, a broadcast and publishing organization. "No one leadership style works in every situation."

Heavner illustrates that with the story of former East Carolina University football coach Sonny Randall, who was a great hero after two straight 9 and 2 seasons at ECU. On the wave of that success, he was recruited by his alma mater, the University of Virginia.

The same techniques that had worked at ECU failed Randall at UVA. In short order, he was no longer the hero.

"What was a very appropriate and productive leadership style at ECU was completely inappropriate at UVA," Heavner pointed out.

What that tells you is that you've got to look beyond the job title that says both these people on your team are sales representatives. You must also understand that one is a family man who is motivated by stability and the other may be a single woman whose goal is to learn as much as possible about your industry in as short a time as possible.

"Too many of the personal goals of people in the corporate sector today are outside their jobs," said Ralston. "It never used to be that way. Always your most important goals were within the job. More and more, the job is a means to an end. The job provides an opportunity for that goal.

"If you as the leader understand that and make suggestions within his personal goal-oriented framework, you're going to get 10 times the amount of effort from that individual."

Individuals. Not teams. It's only by working with individuals that we build them into teams.

Fire In The Belly

As a child, I wasn't known in my own family as one of the hardest workers around.

In fact, if you'd asked older brother Dick, he might've told you how lazy I was. Our family, which grew up in a small North Carolina textile town, had big gardens and some farm animals to tend.

Well, Dick used to milk the cows twice a day, feed the livestock, work in the garden — you couldn't find enough work to fill his day. He flat loved to work.

My only assigned jobs were to feed the hogs and bring

in wood and coal for the stoves and fireplaces. And when I finished those assignments, I have to admit, I didn't go looking for more to do.

Dick, on the other hand, worked until he dropped. I didn't understand that. Until I started working, at the age of 15, at the local radio station. Then, I discovered, I could have worked all day and all night — every day! I didn't even get paid anything the first six months. Nothing. I think I would have paid them for the chance to hang around the station if they'd told me that was how it worked.

What I'd found was something that set my belly on fire. And that, as leaders, is one of our jobs: Setting others on fire with our passion.

Jim Heavner remembers the day he applied for a radio job while still in college at the University of North Carolina-Chapel Hill. Applications were filed by rubber-banding an application around an audition tape and tossing into a big cardboard box. Being a realist, he didn't expect much to happen.

But he remembers the day the station called him, because he feels to this day that the call was his first lesson in setting people on fire with a passion for their work.

"He called and said, 'Wow! You're terrific! We think if you would come to our radio station, you would make us terrific,'" Heavner said, remembering the day. "I'll never forget that day. We all had the idea in those days that you were hired because they had a slot to fill. But I told my mom and dad, 'Not only have they hired me, I think they want me.'

"That guy set me on fire. I would have done anything for him."

(I must blushingly claim to have been party to that

exciting day. Sandy McClamroch, station owner and a mentor of mine, and I first put Jim on the WCHL payroll. For a dollar an hour. We had seven employees. Today, Jim owns the property and has 450 employees! And he recently hired my son, Robert, to work at that same station.)

Jim Heavner truly hasn't forgotten that first experience. Now, when The Village Companies offers someone a job, he takes pride in being able to tell that person that the entire staff voted to make the job offer.

"This gives them a belief that they've been selectively chosen," Heavner said. "We think it's critical to their self-concept, their being willing to fully commit."

He sets them on fire. It's closely related to challenging people, but it goes one step farther.

One of my coaching buddies sees it as the leader's ability to see something in a goal that the rest of the crowd doesn't see.

"It's like the old Mickey Rooney and Judy Garland movies," he said. "They look over and see the barn and everybody else sees a dirty barn. But the leader sees it as a possibility to build a dance hall and have a great musical.

"The leader's the one who did that — it might take carpenters, electricians and other people to make that happen. But the leader is the person who has the ability to bring about that passion in others."

Once you've got fire in the belly, the actions that accompany attitude fall into place much more easily.

Next: Taking Action to Build Your Team

"One of the most profound changes in business is the lack of identity people have with the companies for which they work. And the resultant attitude among the workforce that they're putting in time rather than working for a joint goal."

- Dieter Tannenberg
Sargent-Welch
Scientific Company

ACTION: PARTNER TO ATTITUDE

4

Some of us have pieced together the good, the bad and the ugly of leadership simply by watching others get it all wrong.

One of Tom Carpenter's most vivid lessons came from his first job with Aetna Life & Casualty, when he was about 21. He started out as an underwriter in Hartford, Connecticut. Carpenter remembers clearly what happened everytime he approached his boss, a man nearing retirement, with a question about how to handle a situation.

"He would go over and pull out a drawer and he would look in an envelope and he would answer the question and close his drawer," Carpenter recalled. "All he ever told me or taught me was in response to a direct question — he obviously thought that his power over me was his knowledge.

"In other words, if he knew something and I didn't, that meant he was in charge."

Fortunately for Carpenter, who is now a senior vice president at Aetna, what he learned from that was not to follow this fellow's example.

I'd also wager that Carpenter never felt a bond with this first boss. The two were never on the same team — that's how different the times were then.

Tom's story is a terrific example of how attitude and action work together to influence the team spirit in your department, your sales force, your company. We've talked a lot about attitude: being positive, showing that you care, infusing others with the passion that burns in you.

Now, I want us to talk about the partner to attitude: Action.

Action is the manifestation of attitude. So the actions you take, the concrete things you do to foster a team spirit in your operation, must reflect the kinds of attitudes we discussed in Chapter Three.

To begin, let's break action down into three different categories:

1. Employee needs
2. Communication
3. Empowerment

Now let's take each of those areas and, as we did in the last chapter, discuss specific things you can do to build stronger bonds with the people on your team.

Employee Needs

Jim Heavner with The Village Companies, who told us what he learned about "fire in the belly" from one of his first job offers, also had a good experience on the "hiring" end of a job interview.

Heavner was still at WCHL, this time interviewing a

young man who had worked for him during his college years and was now back looking for another job. Heavner took the young man to lunch and asked him what he had learned in the years since college.

In his big disk jockey voice, this young man told Heavner, "Oh, I know, it's people. When you become program director and you're in charge of people, you find it's really a complicated thing. You've got to worry about people's problems and families and kids and finances and a whole lot of squirrely stuff that doesn't have anything to do with music and news and records and playlists and music mix."

Heavner was impressed. He was even more impressed a few minutes later when the young man told him the area in which he still had the most to learn were his people skills.

"I don't know if he realized what wisdom he was demonstrating," Heavner said.

Understanding our people problems may be one of the biggest challenges leaders face — whether they're in sales or service or manufacturing or finance. And it's only getting harder.

In a major story on its Sunday business pages, The Charlotte Observer recently wrote that companies are likely to take more of an interest in employee's personal lives in the 1990s.

But the motives, said the story, are not entirely altruistic. Corporate profits are at stake.

"Faced with the dilemma of a shrinking labor pool and an increasing dependence on women workers, companies will find that they must be more flexible in accommodating employees," wrote Observer business reporter Karen Lands. "They'll be increasingly faced with such issues as child care, elderly care, home-based work and nontraditional work schedules."

Banker Hugh McColl, who is certainly known for aggressively expanding his market, also feels he's been aggressive in developing programs that make NCNB a good place to work. In fact, Working Mother magazine in 1989 named NCNB one of America's 60 best companies for working mothers.

"We have things like paternity leave, not just maternity leave, and things like flexible work weeks and so forth," said McColl, who recently committed up to $1 million a year to pay half of child care costs for employees with household income of $24,000 a year or less. "The single most important part of leadership is understanding the needs of your followers and providing for them. It seems to me caring about your people is the number one thing."

Jim Jensen points out that, because women have held key positions with his organization for many years, 3-M has taken concrete steps to solve some of the problems inherent in the Supermom syndrome.

The company maintains a liaison with all the day care facilities in its metropolitan area — which ones are good, which ones are marginal, which ones specialize in certain areas.

"Another way we've tried to respond is with our sick child program," Jensen said. "If your child is ill and can't go to day care, we will have a qualified medical person go to your home and take care of that child for a day or week or whatever it takes. The employee still pays day care costs, but the company picks up everything over the regular day care costs."

What does that action say — loud and clear — about the attitude at 3-M?

A personalized work schedule at 3-M also allows

flexible hours whenever the job permits it.

"It's helped a lot of our people," Jensen said. "I have a number of cases in my organization where both husband and wife work here. In one case, the wife may come in at 6:30 and the husband will get the kids off to school. Then she'll be home to catch them coming home from school.

"We, as a company, are responding to those needs in a very positive way, partly because it's a nice thing to do societally. But also because it's good business. It relieves our people from the stress of those problems and allows them to concentrate on the job."

Giving workers some degree of control over the blend of personal with professional lives is one of the ways Southern Shows, Inc., demonstrates a concern for employee needs. President Joan Zimmerman, as fair and empathetic a leader as you'll find anywhere, respects her people at the same time she demands a great deal from them. She insists that her people grow and perform at their best — yet balances that with a sincere concern for their personal needs.

"If they need a day off to go to the beach with their kids, they can make it up any time," said Zimmerman. "They can come in early in the morning or work Saturdays when their husbands or wives are at home with the kids. It's easier for small companies to be that flexible."

But the significant thing about Zimmerman's flexibility is that she isn't the decision-maker when it comes to working out who's going to be off and when they're going to make up the time — the employees are.

"I always tell the person to be sure their co-workers can cover for them on a given day," Zimmerman said. "That gets two people involved. They clear it with each other."

Another family-related issue raised in The Observer is

care for the elderly. According to the Conference Board, an international business research and consulting network, 25-33% of a typical company's employees now care for aging relatives.

The July 16, 1990, issue of Newsweek coined the phrase The Daughter Track, pointing out that the average American woman can now expect to spend an average of 17 years raising children — and an average of 18 years helping aging parents. And people who must care for aging parents or other elderly dependents often use company time confering with doctors, locating home health care, selecting a nursing home and other necessary duties. As a result, some companies are getting actively involved in solutions.

"Today's stressful environment is key," said Knight-Ridder's Dot Ridings. "We're dealing with things today that my parents wouldn't have dreamed of. Emotional stress, time pressures, drug pressures, relationship pressures.

"I'm really glad both the last places I've worked had very good employee assistance plans. I'd like to see more emphasis given to that, because people need help in dealing with their lives today. And that isn't going to go away."

Addressing employee needs also means understanding employee wants. A Conference Board survey of 216 major U.S. companies identified the following criteria as important recruiting tools for the workers of tomorrow:

• Compensation geared to performance, identified by 62%
• Flexible work schedules, 59%
• Flexible benefits, 55%
• Awards/recognition for achievement, 52%
• Opportunity for advancement, 48%
• Atmosphere of employee/employer loyalty, 38%
• Assurances of employment security, 19%

Another important motivator for many workers today is growth. Opportunity. Education. And it's an area in which businesses must begin to accept some responsibility.

If I've hired a $500-a-week person in January and they're still a $500-a-week person in December, something is wrong. I've either hired the wrong person or — and this is much more likely — I've miserably failed my year as a leader.

Workers will feel better about themselves — and do a better job for you — if you let them know that their growth is important to you. If you let them know they are valuable enough to the company that it's worthwhile to invest in their growth.

Our workers are, to steal a wonderful notion from John Fox, our social capital. And social capital will pay huge dividends in loyalty, in productivity and in quality if we are willing to make an investment.

"The key to success is to surround yourself with good people and help them grow," said Coach Bill Foster. "Realistically, I tell everybody who works for me that if they come in and do a heck of a job, they shouldn't be here long. That way they know you want them to move up the ladder."

Encourage your people to learn. Create an environment that makes it easy for them to go across town or across the country for a seminar that will lead them to greater accomplishments. Establish tuition funds for those who want more college training. Consider an on-going, in-house staff development operation.

Jim Tunney said it better than most of us: "We must look at education as a quest, much like the quest for excellence. I don't think anybody becomes excellent and then they stop. Excellence is a quest and it grows as the quest for excellence grows. Learning is a quest, it grows as you grow.

"The more you learn, the more you are able to learn."

No one could slow down a company made up of people who think like that.

Communication

Dieter Tannenberg told me that anyone who can communicate well and listen well is a hero.

I must say I have to agree with Tannenberg, who is CEO of Sargent-Welch Scientific Company. Every single key to leadership that you and I have talked about so far and will talk about before we're finished with this book — every single one of them is linked to communication.

You can't create change successfully without successfully communicating the whys and hows of that change. You can't meet the needs of your employees without communicating the benefits you're putting in place. If nobody knows you've got a "just do it" attitude, will it really make a difference in the production room and the board room and on the sales floor?

Of course not. You've got to communicate if you expect to lead.

"Leadership is...having a vision, communicating that vision to the people you want to bring along and motivating people to go beyond the normal," Tannenberg said. "That to me is leadership."

That could just as easily have been a quote from a dozen other leaders I interviewed. I doubt if any of us could argue with the notion that at the heart of leadership is not only having the vision, but being able to communicate that vision.

Most of us, however, when we approach the task of communication, forget the first and most important step. It isn't writing. Or talking. Or getting that newsletter out on time. It isn't meetings and memos.

The first step to communicating is listening. Listening. And sometimes I think it's the part most of us do worst.

We're fired up with a vision. We have the plan in our sights. We're eager to move down the road toward creating reality out of dreams. But we're not listening. Or we're half-listening while we skim the last page of the report we need to finish before the 2 p.m. meeting. Or we're hearing what we want to hear.

"Leaders are often bright, they're obsessed, they're moving forward, they're on a fast track," said speaker and trainer Chris Hegarty. "They don't realize they must slow down to help somebody else catch the vision."

They don't slow down and listen. I have to confess, I'm sometimes as guilty as anyone. Last night, my wife, Pat, and I were having a very involved conversation. I happened to be reading the newspaper when the conversation started and put it down in front of me. Every once in a while, my eye would wander back down to the paper.

Soon, Pat was asking me — and rightly so — why I kept reading the paper when we needed to have this important conversation.

Don't be guilty of that kind of listening, which clearly communicates to others that something else holds more importance for you than what is being said.

Don Thoren told me about his daughter, Katie, who at 12 decided she wanted to be a marine biologist. Thoren hoped to help her with that goal by coaching her on the need to improve her grades in science and math. But his attempts at leading her to better study habits weren't successful.

Katie kept pointing out that she was only in the seventh grade. She had plenty of time. She didn't need to study those things until she got to college.

Top-notch leader that he is, Thoren realized he was doing something wrong. So he started asking his daughter a series of questions. Why did she think she could wait to study math and science? How many colleges did she think offered the study of marine biology? And how did one get approval to study marine biology once in college?

What he learned, in listening to her answers, was that she believed every college taught marine biology. And that she would be allowed to study it simply because she had, in elementary school and junior high, been allowed to study whatever she wanted simply by signing up for the course.

She hadn't understood that college was a whole new ball game.

"The moral of this story is that I had been talking to her about her actions without ever understanding her beliefs," Thoren said. "Once I understood the beliefs behind the actions, I now had the opportunity to assert some real leadership in her life. Only as I am able to bring her information that changes her beliefs can I expect her to act differently."

So Thoren's advice is to quit fighting people over what they're doing and try to find out why they're doing it.

And the best way to get that information is to listen. "As carefully as we listen to the needs of our customers, we must also listen just as carefully to the needs of our employees," said Bostik President John Fox.

Shintaro Ishihara, a Japanese politician who gained some notoriety with his opinions on American business, said American managers don't listen to their workers. They often move up the ranks never knowing what it's like to work on the factory floor.

I'd like to suggest that you and I listen to Thoren and Ishihara and make sure we're including that first all-important step in our communications plan.

The second major component of good communication is availability.

We have to be there. People must be able to reach us with their ideas. They must know, by how available we are, that we welcome them.

One of the leaders I interviewed said he's been in his position for 22 years and, during that time, he's had the door to his office closed twice.

"In my building, all the senior people have glass windows between them and the outside and they all pull the curtains," he said. "The day I got here, I opened my curtains. I want people to look in because I want to look out — communication is two- way."

Commodore Computer VP Lloyd Mahaffey and Jim Jensen with 3-M are also big backers of the open door philosophy of communication, as is Dr. Tom Haggai with IGA.

"The key to my performance is my executive secretary," Dr. Haggai said. "And that person should never be in the dark. I leave a door open so they can hear everything I'm saying. And if they don't hear all they need to know, they ask."

That points up the very important attitude behind an open-door philosophy.

Great leaders understand that secrets are dangerous.

The more you can share the good news and the bad news with your people, the more ownership they have in the company, the project, the product, the service.

So you have to keep everyone well-informed, up and down and laterally. The fewer secrets you have the better. Obviously, you don't share personal data and individual financial information. But other than that, very little information about your operation should be considered classified. Information empowers people — remember Tom Carpenter's first boss, who carefully hoarded his knowledge and his power — and your goal should be to empower as many of your people as possible.

Even the bad news will create camaraderie. The hows of communication are varied. Perhaps the most important reminder I can give you is this: Each of us retains information differently.

What does that mean, for the leader in you? It means that the memo you labor over, the memo that outlines every detail of the new employee benefits package, won't do the job for everyone in your operation.

Some of us remember the informaton we read best. Others of us need to hear it before we remember it. For still another group, the combination of written and verbal communication is most effective.

So try, if at all possible, to communicate the important stuff in as many different ways as possible. Try to learn how your key people absorb information best. Make sure those same people understand this truth, for the times when they communicate with those who report to them.

Let's look a a couple of top-notch tips on effective ways to communicate.

Meetings are much maligned, but they can be turned into something more than a necessary evil.

They can be effective. They can reach deep and long and uncover the heart of a problem. They can waste as little time as possible.

Allan Hurst plans weekend retreats, which include not only his people, but customers as well. Problems are explored. And the results are taken back and shared with others on the staff.

Bill Foster makes sure every meeting with his coaching staff or his team is necessary and has a specific agenda. "Then you can sit down and have the meeting and everyone knows why you're there and what you're going to cover and how long it's going to take. It's productive."

Haggai said much IGA communication is done through memos, but he is also a great believer in stand-up meetings.

"Our corporate office is not that large in Chicago — we have 33 people or so," Haggai said. "A stand-up meeting is really that. I guess we've had one go on for 30 minutes, but usually they're 10 or 15 minutes."

A college basketball coach with a national reputation for winning discovered that his biggest fault when it came to communicating was procrastinating. He found he busied himself with other things that needed doing and didn't get around to the communicating.

"So what I did was take my calendar and make sure that time for communicating is programmed," he said. "I make sure I fit in time with a player every week and over a 15-week period, I will have talked head to head with everybody."

Let's finish up this section with some thoughts from Bill Yoder, director of employee relations for Duke Power Company, an electrical company with 21,000 employees. Yoder has pulled together what he feels are the five key ingredients to an ideal employee communications plan.

1. **Tell the employee what his or her job is.** Yoder pointed out that this is often overlooked, which results in employees who set their own agenda. In effect, Yoder said, the company then ends up working for the employee.

2. **Tell the employee how he or she is doing.** A task which many find difficult and therefore avoid.

3. **Tell the employee how the work unit is doing.** Employees want to know how their efforts fit into the big picture.

4. **Tell employees how the overall organization is doing.** This is perhaps even more important if the news is bad, when people are most in need of straight talk from the top. People want to know, Yoder points out, how the bad news will affect them as individuals.

5. **Tell employees they are important.** Tell them you care.

Which brings us full circle, from action back to attitude again.

Yoder ends his report this way: "You do not have the option of communicating or not communicating. The only option you have is how well you choose to do it."

Next: The Power of Empowerment

"I'm a Methodist, a reli-gion that has survived 2,000 years because we reaffirm it every Sunday morning. We think it's important for our people to be constantly reaf-firmed in what we stand for."

- Jim Heavner
The Village Companies

THE DECADE OF EMPOWERMENT

5

Joe Dudley Sr., president of Dudley Products, Inc., believes one of the best things he can do as a leader is to work himself out a job.

I like to find a person who thinks that way. As leaders, our job isn't to handle the job, but to empower others to handle the job. To gain buy-in, so that others share our vision and feel — as powerfully as we feel it — fire in the belly for the project.

And I like to find people like Tom Gould, who can also tell you what they're doing about it.

At Younkers, the midwestern department store that is 36 stores strong in five states, CEO Tom Gould has accomplished great things, dollars-and-cents-wise, in the years since he came on the scene. He's turned $500,000 in profits into $14 million in profits in less than five years.

He's accomplished great things, dollars-and-cents-wise, because he realizes how valuable his sales associates are, customer-loyalty-wise.

He does it with extensive training and motivation

programs for sales associates, including a minimum of 16 hours training for sales associates on an on-going basis. He does it with the 30-30 Program — within 30 feet in 30 seconds — a program which encouraged sales associates to promptly recognize customers with a smile and attention.

He does it by having his own stores "shopped" 13,000 times each year, to assure that customers receive the right kind of treatment. He did it with a new compensation program, Satisfaction Plus, which ties employee pay to productivity per hour.

He did it with the Younkers Hall of Fame, which rewards productivity. The 314 associates in the Hall of Fame average $106 an hour in sales.

"If every associate had performed at this level, we would have produced an additional $50 million," Gould said.

Gould is getting close. "In the three years from '86 to '89, we increased the productivity of the average sales associate from $60 an hour to $94 an hour."

And in 1990, he did it with The Year of Empowerment. "We're empowering our sales associates to satisfy the customer at the point of sale," Gould said. "The most critical point when a customer is disappointed with a purchase is when they have to come back to the store. They're already upset. They had to take time and effort to make the return.

"Instead of telling them, 'I can't help you, see the manager,' we're empowering our people to satisfy the customer and ensure that they have a totally satisfying and positive experience.

"It's an opportunity to turn a problem into an opportunity, and we can afford to do it because we have well-trained people."

Younkers may not make a profit on that particular transaction. But that satisfied customer will return — again and again.

The Year of Empowerment. With the kind of results Gould has demonstrated from his efforts to empower his people, maybe we should all agree to label this the Decade of Empowerment.

Establishing Their Own Agenda

Jim Jensen talks about moving into a new position at 3-M and discovering that the food services and vending area was doing an adequate job, but little more.

"We were getting some complaints from our customers and damn few compliments," he said.

Because the manager in that area was nearing retirement, Jensen moved him into a consulting position and himself took responsibility for the food services area. He found a staff of talented people who weren't responding to customer needs because they felt boxed in by the constraints created by the previous manager.

For the next year, Jensen gave that staff the freedom to establish its own agenda.

"They established a very clear vision of where they wanted to go and they were totally empowered to get there," Jensen said. "They were given great flexibility to do new things, experiment, fail, the whole routine.

"That was four years ago and today I would say our food service operation at 3-M is without peer in the country."

Jensen empowered his people — gave them the authority to go with their responsiblity — and they responded with achievement.

Responsibility + Authority = Achievement

That's a powerful equation for those of us who lead. Our greatest power doesn't come from hoarding the power for ourselves. It comes from spreading it around to as many as possible in our operation. It comes from empowering others to do the job they were hired to do.

One of the first steps in that process at 3-M was goal-setting. Jensen didn't present the food services staff with a set of goals. He invited them to set their own goals.

He made them participants in establishing their objectives.

An example of empowerment that most U.S. business leaders would find downright frightening is apparently going on right now in the Soviet Union. Duke University economics professor Thomas H. Naylor, author of "The Gorbachev Strategy," compared the U.S. and Soviet workplaces in a guest column in The Charlotte Observer.

A high degree of trust between employees and managers is absent both in the U.S. and the Soviet Union, Naylor said. And without trust, high levels of productivity are tough to sustain.

"But empowerment is the linchpin of a trusting relationship in the workplace," Naylor wrote. "Without empowerment, there can be no trust. Employees who do not feel empowered by the organization will not internalize the goals, objectives and values of the company.

"To feel empowered, the employee must believe that the managers respect and appreciate their contributions."

Perestroika, he said, is attempting to change that in the Soviet Union, to the degree that in many cases managers must now stand for election by their employees.

Now that's empowerment. There are, however, less radical approaches that work.

Room of Dreams

A coaching friend starts the process in his department by asking each person to prioritize needs for the coming year. Then, he makes every attempt to find a fit between individual goals and organizational goals. And when the fit isn't there, he communicates the reasons, clearly and straightforwardly.

He goes farther than just asking for a wish list, however. He nurtures a feeling that each person in his area has the right to dream.

"We have a room called the room of dreams," he said. "In there, we have a 17-minute tape about dreams that became reality — whether it's the Wright brothers or the first walk on the moon or our hockey team in the Olympics beating the Soviet Union.

"Every once in a while you need a little shot of your dreams. So we go in the room and watch the 17-minute tape and come out rejuvenated!"

One of the most successful leaders I know — Dexter Yager, who heads up one of the world's largest Amway distribution networks — is also a big believer in dreams.

"If your dream is big enough, you'll have the energy," said Yager, who was a $95 per week brewery representative when I first met him. "You have to nourish a dream, feed it, make sure it stays alive and healthy.

"Facts don't count. If the dream is big enough, you change the facts."

Yager, an individualist who represents hundreds of

thousands of distributors worldwide through lineage in his Amway network, is perhaps the best example of how powerful a dream can be.

Coach of the women's basketball team at North Carolina State, Kay Yow, also works closely with individuals in setting goals — academic, athletic, personal.

"I try to help them determine what it is they would really like to have happen, to have said about them, or to have done by the end of the semester or school year," Yow said. "Once we get that down, we try to decide what it will take, what we will have to do to give ourselves our best shot at making that happen. We try to be very specific."

Jim Heavner, as we mentioned before, empowers by making members of the team responsible for recruiting the team. Before hiring, the new person must be approved by each member of the existing team.

Outvoting Their Weak Points

A second thing that must happen in the process of empowering people — and it's tied to the matter of trust that Naylor mentioned — is this business of recognizing their humanity. And the single way that many managers fail that test is in attempting to use intimidation — or fear or withholding of approval, whatever you want to call it — to keep people in line.

You don't keep an empowered worker "in line." An empowered worker is one you've encouraged to raise questions, to disagree with you, to do a little risk-taking of his or her own. That's the kind of worker who becomes a valuable part of the team.

Jim Jensen recalled another situation when he inherited

responsiblity for a department that previously had been managed by intimidation.

"After four or five months, the new manager noticed that one of the key supervisors of the group never offered a creative thought, never had a suggestion, never showed any spark of ingenuity at all," Jensen said.

The manager decided he had to sit down with this supervisor and explain that part of his job was creative thinking. But at the next meeting, this particular supervisor came forth timidly with an idea and the manager's response was, "That sounds great. Take it and run with it."

This supervisor did just that. And did a great job putting his new idea into effect. So instead of having a meeting with this supervisor to ask why he wasn't offering ideas, the manager had one to thank him for the success of his idea. After offering the praise, the manager asked why he'd come forth with no ideas until then.

The supervisor's answer tells us all we need to know about what management by intimidation accomplishes. He said, "For ten years, any time I brought up an idea, it was sneered at, knocked down and I was berated for it. I've been afraid to."

Jensen said this supervisor has turned out to be one of his most creative people. "And yet for ten years, his manager had totally stifled that creativity."

Praise, not criticism — even the best-intentioned, most gently delivered criticism — is a better way to bring out the best in people. And in doing so, you've empowered them to become an active, creative, contributing member of the team.

"What you do is refine people hopefully to their

strengths," said IGA's Haggai. "You try to get their strong points to outvote their weak points. Therefore one of my keys in leading people is praise because you're not going to do any good by criticizing. Even when we say it's constructive, that depends on your ears, not my tongue."

Wally Amos reminded me, too, that we have to remember when we're tempted to criticize that low self-esteem is at the root of many of our "people" problems.

"The biggest obstacle is people who don't believe in themselves, low self-esteem," Amos said. "Low self-esteem is the root cause of just about every social problem and the negative behavior people demonstrate. What they're saying is, 'Hey, pay attention to me. I don't feel I'm worthy.'"

One of the best ideas I've seen for empowering employees, and thus making it impossible for them to be anything but a dynamic, contributing part of the team, is the Shared Values philosophy at Sverdrup, an architectural firm responsible for such legendary structures as the New Orleans Superdome and the Pentagon in Washington, D.C.

Executive Vice President Dick Beumer shared with me their simple 10-page booklet, Shared Values. I'll bet there aren't a thousand words in the whole piece. But it covers everything you need to know about the kind of company Sverdrup is.

As an employee of Sverdrup you will, by the time you finish reading Shared Values, know the cornerstone values upon which the firm was founded and continues to operate. You will know that integrity and keeping commitments are a vital part of the beliefs that bind Sverdrup employees. One page outlines — simply and concisely

— what Sverdrup expects from the company, from the individuals within the company, even from its clients and society as a whole. Another details employees' obligations to each other, to the company and to society.

It's a powerful document that's had powerful results at Sverdrup. It uplifts and empowers.

It's the perfect blending of attitude and action that truly bonds people together and makes them a team.

Next: Who Are Tomorrow's Team Members

"Aside from interest and inflation rates, demographics will be the story in the 1990s."

- David Orr,
Economist
First Union Corporation

HANDLING THE FALL-OUT FROM OUR CHANGING WORKFORCE

6

The headline over the story about a Wall Street Journal survey on life at the top of the corporate ladder caught my eye.

"White, Protestant and Successful"

The survey, the results of which were published about a year ago in "The Wall Street Journal Book of Chief Executive Style," was based on a look at the personal lives and habits of 351 chief executive officers of the nation's biggest companies.

The results shouldn't have surprised me, I suppose. But for some reason they did.

If these 351 corporate leaders are indicative of what's going on across the board in corporate America, most of our leaders are white Protestant men, married to the same woman — who, by the way, stays home — for 20 years. Three children. Served in the armed forces. Mostly college educated.

I couldn't help but notice how off-kilter that group is with the demographics that will dominate the workplace in the decade ahead.

"Aside from interest and inflation rates, demographics will be the story in the 1990s," First Union Corporation economist David Orr told The Charlotte Observer.

To see what he means, take a look at some of the demographic changes that will leave their mark on tomorrow's economy, according to the U.S. Labor Department:

- Almost two-thirds (64%) of the new workers entering the job market during the final decade of this century will be women.
- By the year 2000, three out of five women (61%) of working age are expected to hold paying jobs.
- By the year 2000, nearly half (47%) of the work force will be female.
- Of these working women, three out of five will be mothers. "Almost half of all mothers with children under one year old are working — an amazing change," Labor Secretary Elizabeth Dole said.
- More than half (58%) of the young people entering the work force between now and the year 2000 will be Black, Hispanic or Asian. Unfortunately, many members of these groups have cultural and educational disadvantages that often disqualify them for jobs demanding high skills, according to the Joint Economic Committee of Congress. The reason? Read on.
- 40% of all black teenagers drop out of high school and more than 50% of Hispanic youths fail to graduate.
- The workforce will also be older, with 50% of the workforce made up of people 35 to 54 years old and 11% age 55 and older. In 1988, those figures were 38% and 13%.

Equally alarming information comes to us from the

U.S. Educational Services Department, which said in 1988 that one-third of the nation's population is functionally illiterate. In terms of literacy, the U.S. has dropped to 49th place among the 158 nations of the United Nations.

And in our prisons, 75 percent of our inmates have not completed high school — 40 percent didn't make it beyond the eighth grade.

The impact of these trends? According to the Commission on the Skills of the American Work Force, 70% of non-college, front-line workers (clerks, secretaries, machinists, etc.) "will see their dreams slip away" unless society invests more in improving their skills.

Some of these figures are encouraging — more minorities in the workforce is a goal America has been striving toward for more than three decades. That's the first step toward changing the results of the Wall Street Journal survey, toward creating a workforce and a leadership that can't be labeled by race, sex or religion.

But let's be honest. Some of these figures are anything but encouraging. Higher numbers of people with a so-called "skills gap" is anything but encouraging.

The U.S., economic prognosticators say, is running out of workers who can do the jobs the 1990s will require.

Predictions are that this skills gap could drag down the economy, lower our standard of living, weaken the U.S. in its international competition and create a class of isolated, underprivileged people.

"For the first time since World War II, America is about to enter a period of prolonged labor shortage — a shortage of both workers and skills," said Senator Edward Kennedy, chairman of the Senate Labor and Human Resources committee, in a recent news story.

These aren't very pleasant predictions. And our job, as

the leaders of tomorrow, is to make sure we're equipped to handle the fall-out from this problem.

Washington Post columnist William Raspberry, one of many who have addressed themselves to the implications of these figures, wrote, "What do the numbers mean? ... To employers, they mean the necessity of learning to deal with diversity."

He goes on to say that it means paying a lot more attention to getting traditionally undereducated and underprepared minorities ready to take advantage of the opportunities that will come with the labor shortage.

"Too many of our children are behind from the day they enter kindergarten, because their parents have not imbued them with...'megaskills' — the attitudes, habits and intellectual stimulation necessary for school success," Raspberry wrote. "Too many of our teenagers are leaving school as dropouts, premature parents or criminals, not merely because they are cheated of opportunity but also because we have not made them understand the extent to which their future is in their own hands.

"We have to shift their focus — and ours — away from the still too prevalent impediments and toward the opportunities of which they take too little advantage."

Raspberry's column then challenges minority leaders to teach disadvantaged young people that preparation and application are necessary to take advantage of opportunity.

That isn't a challenge just for minority leaders. It's a challenge for all of us who want to call ourselves leaders. It's a challenge for each of us who want to be part of the Ethics Epidemic.

Let's talk about the steps each of us must take in order to turn our problems into opportunities.

• *Make education your personal priority.* If the biggest problem we face is an underprepared and undereducated work force, the leaders of America must take a leadership role in this problem, also.

And that means more than just initiating a new-product training program or a seminar for upgrading skills once a month. It means starting long before the education reaches your particular bottom line.

"We'd better go back to elementary school," said Wally Amos. "We'd better start working with our young people. We're perpetuating the same system and we're going to have the same breakdowns."

Individually and corporately, we must get involved with America's youth and with America's education system. We must accept responsiblity. We must make a difference wherever we can. We must support solutions with our sweat and with our dollars and with our hearts.

We'll find out how some leaders are doing it in Chapter Nine.

• *Embrace diversity.* If I am a white male — one of the Wall Street Journal types — I must learn to understand and appreciate and work well at the side of Blacks, Hispanics, Asians, women. If you are a Black woman, you must learn to do the same for me.

It is no longer just your job to deal with those who fit your demographic profile, according to Ciba-Geigy Director of Human Relations Mae Douglas.

"There was a time when a lot of people felt, because I am Black, that my role was to uplift the rest of the Blacks in this organization," she said. "And I resented that. I have to make sure everybody is treated fairly."

The melting pot idea has to become more than a platitude. It has to become the way we live. This nation teeters dangerously on the brink of a new racism. A racism that threatens to be more virulent, more violent, than anything we saw on the streets of American in the 1960s.

Can we, as the leaders of American business, combat that with a value system that says we **can** work together? **Will** work together. **Must** work together. Can the American work ethic become the common ground that will bind us together when our ethnic heritage has kept us apart?

I believe it can. But this, like so many of the things we've discussed, starts with the individual. Must become institutionalized. Must become part of the philosophy we put to work in our board rooms, our assembly lines, our shipping docks.

"We've always felt that the solution to the problem lies somewhere else," said Robert Stark, Executive Vice President for Hallmark Cards. "There is a lack of acceptance of responsibility, a failure to recognize that the only person I'm likely to change is me.

"Change starts with me." We must go beyond understanding the needs of the women in our workforce — child care and elder care and the lack of role models. We must go beyond understanding the needs of racial minorities in our workforce — lack of education and an acculturation that sets them apart from those who call the shots.

We must go beyond those labels to understanding the needs of the individuals.

Look hard at the demographic information in this chapter. Memorize the trends. Be alert to changes in those trends. Then remember that this information is simply numbers. And we're talking about people.

The person who keeps your equipment running smoothly isn't just a black male with 10.2 years of education and 3.2 children at home. He's a man who wants to spend more time at home while his children are still young. Or she's a woman who spends her off-hours in classes, in the hopes of giving her children a better life. Or he's a man who worries that his oldest son is falling in with the wrong crowd.

And how successfully you work with that person is going to depend on how effectively you focus on who that person is.

Next: The Three Ps of Managing Your Success

"Happiness is an inside job."

- Joe Dudley Sr.
Dudley Products Inc.

MANAGING SUCCESS: PRESSURE, POWER AND PERFECTIONISM

7

You and I both know what all too often comes with success. Ulcers. Heart attacks. Divorce. Lots of business associates but few you'd call a friend when the need for one arises. Alienation from the very people for whose sake you wanted to succeed: your spouse, your children.

Often, success brings with it the kind of rewards we can do without. It robs us of many of the things that make life worth living. If we aren't careful, we wake up one morning alone — emotionally if not in actuality.

We've talked a lot about our responsibilities to those who work for us, to those who take their orders from us and rely on us to sign their paychecks.

What about your responsibility to yourself? Let's talk for a bit about managing our success, and what we can do to make sure that our success in business doesn't leave us a failure in life.

We're going to look at managing success in five key ways:

- **Balance vs. Passion** — Is it possible to
  have fire in the belly for something without

shortchanging the rest of your life?

- **Believing Your Own Publicity** — Ego is healthy, up to a point. Where does leadership end and craving power begin?
- **Losing Touch** — One of the most dangerous side effects of success is a breakdown in the lines of communication with those who are at the bottom of the ladder you've managed to climb.
- **Becoming a Life-long Learner** — Once you decide you know all you need to know, you've started the gradual downslide that leads right back to the bottom of the heap.
- **Failure** — It's frightening, it's had some bad press, but if you don't do it, you're doing something wrong. Bad wrong.

Balance vs. Passion

I'm a bad one to preach on this subject. I don't even have a hobby. My work is my hobby. Always has been. When I was a young broadcaster, that was my hobby. I could work eight hours, then hang around eight more because I'd rather be there than anywhere else. I never knew when quitting time came.

You won't find many leaders who wouldn't have to plead guilty to the same offense. We all seem to make little distinction between work and play.

"This whole idea of leaping tall buildings, stopping speeding bullets — people say, 'Do you really mean that?'" said Aetna's Tom Carpenter. "And the answer is 'Yes, damn right!'"

For those of us with fire in the belly, work and play are

the same thing.

Now let me take my time at the confessional one step farther. I don't see anything wrong with being what we call a workaholic. I know the doctors and the reformed Type A's and the spouses who are left home to mind the family would gladly line the sidewalk in front of The Cullen Center, picket signs in hand, to let me know how little they appreciate that remark.

But I have to be honest. What separates the leader from the follower is often the passion that won't permit balance.

Someone once said that nothing great was ever accomplished by a balanced person. It takes an obsessive person to accomplish the earth-shattering, the mountain-moving. Leaders must be consumed by their vision, must have a steadfast focus on where they're going.

That viewpoint is so easy to defend it's hardly worth going into. Roosevelt. Ghandi. Golda Meir. Kennedy. King. Mother Theresa. Mandella. Margaret Thatcher. None of them had balance.

But each of them moved mountains. No denying that. And there are millions of people each year who move mountains in their own arenas through that same kind of drive and determination — the top sales person in your company, the local high school quarterback who breaks all the records, the service manager who makes sure everybody's satisfied before he closes up shop every day.

I can't claim to fit well in the company of the Roosevelts and Thatchers of the world, but Pat Boyd all too often complains that she doesn't want her husband to talk about work after hours.

That puts a serious crimp in my after-dinner conversation. It's hard to bank that fire in the belly just because the clock strikes five.

Amway exec Dexter Yager is the perfect example of the successful person who wouldn't give you a nickel for balance.

"A livelihood is made from eight to five," Yager said. "A fortune is made after five."

That's hard to argue with. Now that I've admitted that, let me also encourage you to find some measure of balance in life. Because no matter how passionate we are about the part of our life we call our business, we owe it to ourselves to find ways to be passionate about the other parts of our lives.

And that is the key. Don't give up the passion; spread it around.

Search for an awareness of the other aspects of your life: physical, spiritual, mental, family. Look for ways to give them weight, to make yourself a fuller, more complete human being by sometimes remembering that there is life after the board meeting.

My friend and fellow consultant Don Thoren from Phoenix did that by becoming as obsessive about other aspects of his life as he is about his work.

"The things that I do in my personal life are things that require total concentration," Thoren said. "Otherwise, my professional life is so all-consuming that I carry it with me everywhere I go.

"Two of my personal activities are riding motorcycles and doing downhill skiing. If you're not paying attention to what you're doing, either one of those can be dangerous. And because they require total concentration, I find when I have finished with those activities, my mind has really been rested, that I've truly been away from my professional life."

That's terrific advice from someone who's clearly learned that it's even possible to be obsessive about balance — and to use that to advantage.

Allan Hurst thinks of outside activities as a way to — in his words — bring fresh water into a brackish swamp. That points up a good lesson for us all. If we're so wrapped up in one part of our life, it's possible we may eventually bring nothing to our work — no originality, no enthusiasm, none of that passion we need so desperately when it comes time to motivate others. So try Hurst's suggestions — exercise, run, talk, laugh, listen to a tape, write a letter, call a friend.

"Get out of your own circle, or let something into your circle so you can see some new perspective," Hurst said.

Balance is such an important issue for my friend Jim Babb, former President of Jefferson-Pilot Communications, that he makes a point of telling his employees — and their spouses — that the company isn't important enough to sacrifice family time day in and day out.

Jefferson-Pilot operates TV stations in Charlotte, NC, and Richmond, VA, as well as radio stations in five major markets and media-related operations worldwide.

But Babb, now Chairman of Outlet Television, is such a believer in the importance of family that when he holds his annual meeting for employees, he invites spouses, too. And tells them he wants to know if they ever feel that the company is getting in the way of family life.

One wife took him up on his offer. Her husband's health was suffering, she told Babb, as was his relationship with his four young sons. Babb sent the general manager for a physical exam and learned his only problem was stress.

"I had a meeting with him and told him, 'This job is not that important,'" Babb said. "He had amplified in his own mind what my expectations were. I encouraged him to take his sons with him on his next business trip, and to make time to do things with them."

The search for balance is going to be such an issue in the '90s that Babb believes more time off and longer vacations will be considered a greater reward than more pay. A look at the attitudes of what Time magazine called the twentysomething generation in its July 16, 1990, issue will tell you Babb is probably right. An estimated 40% of people in their 20s are children of divorce. Others were latchkey kids, who had to fend for themselves at a fairly young age because both parents worked.

And 64% of them told Time that they wanted to spend more time with their own children. One young woman went so far as to predict that her generation would be known as the family generation. And they're willing to sacrifice the climb to the top to get the satisfaction they want out of life.

Perhaps when that generation moves into the board rooms, balance won't be the problem it is today. But for most of us, the '90s will bring more of the same: more things to do than there are hours in the day.

Jim Jensen at 3-M demonstrates the true achiever's approach to balance. He breaks his life into three categories —work, family and civic — then uses a technique called solo visioning.

"The first thing each morning, I sit down and ask myself what are the key things I want to accomplish today in each of those three categories," Jensen said. "I put them down and each day make sure I'm devoting some time, some energy, some part of myself to each of those areas.

"When I do that it becomes a matter of time management and that's pretty straightforward."

Managing all those different parts of life become especially important when you're the mother of a seven-year-old and president of one of the largest and most respected community colleges in the nation. Dr. Ruth Shaw, president of Central Piedmont Community College, leads a high-profile, hectic professional life. But her private life, she says, epitomizes the cocooning metaphor of the 1990s.

"I wouldn't say I'm a social recluse, but I'm at the other end of the continuum from a party animal," Dr. Shaw said. "I tend to spend time with family. Even our closest friends tend to be cousins and that kind of thing, so there is no agenda, nothing related to work or professional pressures.

"When I took this job I told the Board, 'If you want somebody who's going to work every night, get yourself another boy. I have a small child and I rarely do evenings.' And I've stuck to that for four years."

Linda Lockman-Brooks, an Account Vice President for American Express Travel-Related Services, was quoted recently saying that the main challenge for women is to achieve the balance found by black women, who have juggled family life and work life for generations.

At the same time, the mother of two gives herself permission not to be Superwoman.

"I believe that you can't get an A in both sides every single day," Lockman-Brooks was quoted. "there are going to be days when I'm going to be a champion out there in the business world, and maybe I'm a B-minus mom that day. And then there will be days where it'll be Bs or Cs across the board.

"I think you have to accept that and realize there are always going to be trade-offs."

However you decide to handle the issue of balance in

your life, some stress will surface. Hurst's suggestions will work for some of us. But for being plain old honest about dealing with stress, I like what was said by Harvey Gantt, a Charlotte architect who served as mayor for a number of years and recently attracted national attention in his bid to oust long-time U.S. Senator Jesse Helms.

When things get rough, Gantt admitted with a laugh, he's as likely to slam a fist on the table as anything else. "I used to call tennis stress management by going out and slamming a ball and letting myself get engrossed in a game of tennis."

Most of the time, however, Gantt lets his ethics free him of too much pressure.

"I always felt that as long as your decisions are the ones you can live with personally, then you're not going to feel as much pressure," Gantt said. "Being able to sleep at night is a measure of stress management."

Believing Your Own Publicity

What ego needs is a good P.R. person. Ego, over the years, has received a lot of bad press. Most of it undeserved. As leaders, we wouldn't be where we are were it not for ego, if not for our healthy respect for self. If we didn't have confidence in our vision, in our abilities, in the value of our ideas, we would leave the leading to someone else.

Ego is the starter button for our inner drive. Without that, we would never step front and center. What's happened, I suspect, is that we've allowed ourselves to confuse ego — our sense of self — with egotism. False pride. Bravado. Actually, the person who is most insecure, who feels the most inadequate, may manifest his or her screaming ache as great bravado and self-aggrandizement.

What gets us in trouble is not our ego. It is this egotism, this false pride, this business of believing our own good press.

One of the best ways I know to avoid that is to keep a sharp lookout for your own weaknesses as a leader, as an individual. Weaknesses. Shortcomings. We've all got them. I've certainly got my share.

One of mine is a bad one. I'm long on planning and talking and thinking and short on execution. Just acknowledging that helps me, to an extent, overcome it. I know I have to put more emphasis on execution just to get a thing done.

If I know my weakness, I can find a way to overcome it. If I won't admit my weakness, it will surely find a way to overcome me.

Allan Hurst says one of his roles as a leader is not only acknowledging his own warts, but also exposing them to those who follow him. "They don't see as many as I know I have, but the ones they do see, they feel they can comment on. That's what I do to keep the communication going in our company."

What happens when you can't or won't see your weaknesses? Your ego, the self-esteem that encourages you to lead others toward whatever vision motivates you, moves out of the healthy realm and threatens to become a hunger for power.

LSU basketball coach Dale Brown feels many leaders are so drunk with power they've forgotten their own transgressions and weaknesses.

"A lot of people are afraid of leaders because they think leaders don't have flaws," Brown said. "You could talk to the former coach and principal at my high school, Father Hogan, about temptation or sex or whatever and he would always share the truth. There was never a barrier. He always made himself transparent to you."

You can only be that honest if your ego is healthy enough to allow you to admit your weaknesses. We all need to get there to be the most effective leaders. Otherwise, we're fooling ourselves as much as we're fooling anyone else. We're what Brown calls a counterfeit leader.

"Most leadership is counterfeit, phoney, charlatan," he said. "The world is looking for leaders. An illuminating example of how people are searching is all these counterfeit evangelists they're following. That's a perfect example that people want to be lead.

"Everyone on this earth is searching for peace and love and happiness and success. We don't need a batallion or a regiment to get us there. We need leaders."

Losing Touch

Japanese politician Ishihara spotted it. UNC-Charlotte basketball coach Jeff Mullins spotted it. You've probably seen plenty of good examples yourself. Now it's time to do something about it.

"The executive branch in a large corporation can be too far removed from the business they're in," Mullins said. "I was in the automobile business with General Motors and I felt like the upper levels had no clue what was going on on the street with their products.

"This was when they were introducing diesels. They had this poor product, but rather than having a problem-solving mentality they had more of a cover-your-behind mentality. Don't let the next manager know we've got this problem. Keep it here."

Consequently, he said, layers of covering up problems kept managers too far removed from the business they were in.

How can we avoid this danger of losing touch with the reality of our business? It's a tough balancing act, with no clear-cut rules. A few guides through the underbrush might include:

• *Taking frequent inventory.* Don't rely too heavily on the status quo. Constantly look for places where complacency might be settling in, where the comfort level is so high it's discouraging change.

One of the best ways I've heard for doing that comes from Lloyd Mahaffey, who created a plan called The Good, The Bad and The Ugly, first at Apple Computer, then at Commodore Computers.

Once a year, he takes members of the organization off-site and breaks them into small groups, led by someone who is not a manager. Managers don't get to participate.

"I ask each of those groups to answer three questions," Mahaffey said. "What are those things we do really well and should continue doing. They only get to list five. Then, what are those things we do okay, but we really should do a lot better? Then, what shouldn't we do at all because they're debilitating the organization."

The reports are consolidated into a slide show for the entire organization.

"It's like a whole-group therapy session," Mahaffey said. "The managers don't know who said what, so everybody's safe. But the managers have to face, in a full forum, the goods, the bads and the uglies.

"The interesting thing about The Good, The Bad and

The Ugly is that the first time you do it, the uglies are real ugly. The bads are pretty bad and the goods are okay. The second time you run it, the uglies are more like bads, bads are more like goods and the goods are phenomenal.

"So what you do is begin to flush all major barriers to success."

Doesn't it make you wonder what The Good, The Bad and The Ugly would be in your organization?

• *Having hard-nosed advisors.* Especially advisors who aren't merely reflecting what you want to hear. Those of us who plow ahead often don't seek out other opinions. Indeed, most leaders go against the tide. But we must be willing, eager, to surround ourselves with a hoard of "no-men" so we don't come so close to believing our own publicity. So we are forced to constantly evaluate and defend the decisions we're making.

Good leaders welcome that, as Bostik's John Fox learned from his first boss.

Fox's first boss said to him, 'You know, so many people agree with me all the time. But you (Fox) don't do that. It drives me crazy when you disagree with me. But at the same time, I have to have someone who disagrees with me or I just don't know where I stand. I don't know if my ideas are good or not if someone doesn't challenge me."

• *Becoming part of the universe.* You've got to be able to circumvent the usual lines of communication. Spend time on the assembly line, with the minimum-wage workers. You've got to be out there on the firing line, listening to your people. Be accessible. Listen.

And most important, let them know you're willing to hear the bad as well as the good. Once you have the reputation for shooting the messenger who bears the bad news, you'll always be the last to know what's really going on in your company.

"I think everyone realizes the best ideas usually come from the bottom of the organization, not the top," said Fox. "Stay close to the people who can make things happen and leadership gets very easy."

Great leaders knock out the executive dining room and build long tables with lots of chairs, for cross-pollenation. Leaders can have lunch there and get some good intelligence, build some bonds. Scheduling lunch with people other than your golfing cronies, riding to the meeting in the next town with people other than the ones you normally see. That will get you started on building a good feedback system.

• *Asking the customer.* This is the best lesson we can learn from leaders in the sales profession: Spend time with the customer. The customer will tell you what you really need to hear. If you establish that relationship, you can stay in pretty good touch with the things you ought to be hearing.

Life-long Learning

You'll find no better way to hang onto your perspective than by remembering that you'll always be no better than a student of your profession.

It's hard to let your ego get out of hand when you're willing to admit that every day offers the opportunity for you to learn something new.

"The concept of continuous improvement, the idea that whatever it is we do, we are capable of doing better — if we accept that as the norm, it's a joy rather than a challenge," said Robert Stark with Hallmark Cards.

We must incorporate that image of ourselves as lifelong learners into our image of ourselves as leaders. It's essential for our personal well-being. It's crucial for our professional well-being. And it's one of the best ways to lead by example that I can think of — if those who work with you see you constantly moving ahead, opening yourself to new ideas, they'll most certainly follow your lead.

Tom Carpenter said one of the reasons leaders fail is that they stop learning at some point.

"I used to work for a guy who said it this way: 'When you stop getting better, you stop being good,'" the Aetna exec said. "There's a lot to that."

Some thoughts about the best ways to become a lifelong student of your profession — and how to encourage that in your co-workers.

• **Work on your weaknesses.** We've already admitted we've got them. So once you've figured out what they are, go to work on them. Conquer them. Turn those weaknesses into strengths.

"Public speaking was always extremely difficult for me," said Coach John Ralston. "Yet if I was going to ascend to a leadership role, it was something I had to do so I went and worked at it."

Presentation skills. Computer literacy. Knowledge of marketing. Negotiation skills. Performance evaluations. Wherever you find your individual shortcomings, find a way to improve them. Workshops. Seminars. College classes. A day at the library. Practice.

Whatever it takes, work on your weaknesses.

• **Look for opportunities to grow.** Make it your business to build in time for professional growth. Read more. Listen more. Ask questions.

"I was sitting next to a librarian on a plane and the

librarian told me that if you read about two books a year, you're going to be in the top ten percent of the people who read in this country," said a coach friend of mine. "That's unbelievable. So I started reading about 70 pages a day, seven days a week. That's 400 pages a week, which is a book a week, which means you're going to read 50 books a year."

I've made much the same vow to myself. I can't say I'm as successful as my friend seems to be. But making reading a part of my daily routine forces me to expand my horizons on a regular basis.

• **Seek out teachers.** Dr. Tom Haggai made one of the best suggestions I've heard. Some of us gravitate toward crowds where we'll be the center of attention, the one others look up to. That's natural. But Haggai pointed out that becoming one of the followers from time to time will make us better leaders.

"I have made a conscious effort to associate with people who challenge me, rather than people I might challenge," he said. "I don't feel the least bit intimidated by being around people who are smarter than I."

How can you help but grow if you place yourself in the path of great ideas, great minds?

Dr. Jim Tunney with the NFL wraps it up pretty well. "Better than you were yesterday but not as good as you will and can be tomorrow."

That brings us to the final point in our discussion of managing success. And it deserves a chapter of its very own, because fear of it is what often keeps us from true success.

Next: Failure

---

*"Some pople make excuses;
other people make money."*

*- Dexter Yager
Entrepreneur and
Amway Executive*

FAILING YOUR WAY TO SUCCESS

8

"You're going to be the next Johnny Carson."

Until I hit the age of 35 — a time when reality often begins to put a bit of a tarnish on some of our dreams — I truly expected someone to bound up on a white charger, scoop me up and make that announcement.

I wanted to be a star. And I worked at it. During the Mike Douglas talk show era of the '60s, I tried to organize a syndicated show through my company, Jefferson Pilot Broadcasting. I substituted for Arthur Godfrey on CBS. During the national search that discovered Merv Griffin, I was one of the TV personalities who received some consideration. I did a national CBS feed for a Thanksgiving parade and, later, with Tom Bosley and Cleo Laine was the TV host for the 1976 Bicentennial celebration from Washington.

But you've probably realized that I didn't make it to Carson's slot. He's managed to get along fine with very little worry about whether I'm waiting in the wings to unseat him.

So you might say I failed at that dream. But what I

learned, along the way to figuring out what stalled my accomplishment of that dream, has helped me avoid similar failures.

I failed at that dream because, although I pursued it in what had seemed like a whole-hearted way, I had pursued it without a plan. It was just dreams. I never structured it into a plan. So talent aside, there was very little chance of my succeeding at that.

Setting the goal was no guarantee I'd make it. However, not setting the goal did guarantee little likelihood of achieving it.

The experience wasn't entirely wasted effort, however. I learned the urgency of having goals, and not just dreams.

So out of that failed dream grew the seed that eventually enabled me to establish goals, to develop a strategy for meeting those goals. In failing, I learned to succeed.

Viewed in that light, not making a particular dream come true seems not so much failure as it is a necessary step in the process of becoming a success.

Paralyzed by Fear

I talk a lot to high school groups, young people. That's one of my great joys, to be asked to meet those fresh young people with their eyes full of stars. They've all set their sights on the Big Dream.

What I like to tell them is that it's okay to fail. What's not okay is to be average by default. To quit. To give up.

In most things, you fail your way to success. So failing is more than just okay, it's part of the experience you need to get you to the top. There isn't a profession that's fail-proof. You can't make a single decision that's fail-proof. Failure is as much a part of the mix as success. People who have persistence, who understand that failure is part of the formula, get a lot more distance than those who view failure as a plague to be avoided at all costs.

Because when we view failure in that way, the result is most often an inertia born of fear. Fear of failure is one of the great fears. Most of us, rather than fail, will not use an average skill. We won't take the chance because of fear of ridicule, scorn, rejection.

So, paralyzed by fear, we do nothing. And, as we discussed in Chapter One, that's a quick way to work yourself out of your position of leadership. Leaders must act. Leaders must decide.

Leaders must take risks. Even if it means chalking up an occasional failure.

Four years ago, after his stroke, doctors told Amway exec Dexter Yager he would never get out of a wheelchair.

"But I fought my way out," said Yager, who also fought his way to the top from some pretty humble beginnings. "I still drag a leg and one arm doesn't work too good, but I decided not to be a wimp."

Yager pointed out that a reading of Forbes will tell you that many of the most successful people in America were originally from poor or middle-class background — they were born into what most of us would call failure.

"They had to deal with a lot of rejection," Yager said. "But they decided not to be rejected any more. I wasn't the best-dressed kid in school and I fought to earn my own acceptance. Everybody who's highly successful got kicked in the teeth."

But they didn't accept the label of failure. They took

action to reverse the label.

So a true leader must learn to use failure, to see it as a benchmark, a guideline, a way to judge progress. But not as a deterrent. The risk-taking that goes along with riding the crest of change, according to IGA Chairman Tom Haggai, becomes a trial by fire for leaders. You'll remember his quote from Chapter One.

"Until you risk everything, until you get to that point in life where you face losing everything — and overcome the fear — you're never going to lead."

We do it by accepting that risk makes some failure inevitable. In others. In ourselves.

Playing It Safe

Leaders with whom I've spoken about change have pointed out that one thing we have to change is our attitude about failure. If we actively pursue change, if we are committed to shaking out of it every bit of growth and innovation we can, we are going to fail.

But don't allow yourself — or others — to translate failure into personal defeat.

"I know people who are marvelously creative, but the reason they never lead is they don't have the courage to act upon that which they create," Haggai said. "Leaders have the vision and the courage to act and thus don't even think in terms of success or failure. They believe even failure becomes the stepping stone for the next achievement."

Eddie James, president of a Louisville advertising company, takes an equally pragmatic approach to what many label failure.

"My wife runs a successful company and she'll ask sometimes if I think she should do this or that," James said. "My answer to that is, 'Do it and if it doesn't work, don't do it any longer.'"

Sounds like a simplistic approach; and maybe it is. But the fact of the matter is, both James and Haggai are right. You must have the courage to follow your instincts, to reach for the next goal. You must be willing to overreach yourself sometimes. Willingness to take action is a key ingredient for the real leader.

Because success isn't born out of failure by chance. You have to make it happen.

"I don't like the term luck," said Yager. "Luck is a loser's excuse for a winner's effort and commitment. Failure doesn't happen unless you allow it."

If you can remember that there's dignity in trying, you will go far. Some of us don't allow ourselves that dignity because we're too afraid of being judged by others. We'd rather play it safe by playing it perfect.

"Most people are afraid to fail, so if they do something that isn't right, it either destroys them or they deny that they failed or they blame someone else," said Coach Dale Brown. "If I do a poor job, I'll take the blame. I have a great failure quotient. It's not your IQ, it's your FQ."

Another coach I interviewed, Kay Yow with N.C. State's women's basketball program, said one of the worst traits leaders have is that refusal to admit to their own mistakes.

"That's a killer, this inability leaders have to be wrong," Yow said. "When a person has that kind of attitude, it puts them on the defensive if you ask a question. They immediately perceive it as a threat to them, some kind of weakness in them."

The weakness, of course, is only in how the failure is handled and not in the failure itself.

Permission to Fail

It's time we learned to regard failure as an opportunity offered, not an opportunity missed. A sales person who failed, then quit, would not be a sales person. An athlete who lost and didn't compete again wouldn't be an athlete.

So the true lesson here is that failure is only meted out when you quit. It isn't failure until you quit.

Once you realize what a paralyzer fear is, and give yourself permission to try — and even fall short of the goal — you've already created one success for yourself. Because once you've done the thing you fear, it will be yours. Half the world is traumatized into inaction simply because they will not live by that axiom.

One of our favorite activities at Ty Boyd Enterprises is our monthly Executive Speaker Institute (ESI), an intensive training session on presentation and speaking skills. We do it out of our homebase, Charlotte, as well as in major cities nationwide. ESI is dear to our hearts, and not solely because it allows us to share with others something that we love.

What is truly special about ESI is what happens to the people who walk through our two-and-a-half day trial by fire.

You've probably heard, as I have, that fear of speaking in public is the number one fear in America. We fear public speaking more than we fear death. So we know, when we open the doors for ESI each month, that we're going to greet a dozen people who approach us with fear and loathing. They'll have sweaty palms. A racing pulse. Dry mouth. In a case of fight or flight, they're definitely leaning toward flight — if only their knees would stop shaking long enough.

But they walk through the door. They accept the challenge. They resolve to look foolish, if that's what it takes. Because they are committed to conquering their fear of public speaking.

And what happens is so exciting that it invariably becomes an emotional experience for everyone.

They leave ESI feeling that they can conquer not only their fear of public speaking, but anything else that dares to get in their way.

In watching people at ESI every month, I've learned not only how important it is to give myself permission to fail. I've learned that I have to encourage my people to fail. Those who work with me know they're not going to be scolded if they fail. That's much more likely to happen if they don't try.

Because if you're going to get all you can out of people, you've got to give them the freedom to fail.

So what I would tell you is this: Don't stop making mistakes. I hope you make a lot in your business life. Because each mistake is a building block for the next success.

Next: Giving to Your Community

9

"What turned me around was the discovery that I could use the company as a tool...I could change things that I couldn't change on my own. I'd never before equated business with doing anything good, never thought of using it to promote a cause."

- Yvon Chouinard
Patagonia Inc.
(As quoted in Inc. Magazine)

A SHIRT-SLEEVES EFFORT: GIVING BACK TO SOCIETY

One in 11 babies born in this country is born addicted to drugs.

Children of poverty must look too hard to find role models who can point the way to success.

The Styrofoam cup from which we drank our morning coffee at yesterday's seminar will still be around in the year 2300 — assuming the earth will be here at all.

We're arguing louder than ever before for quality education — and graduating fewer students every year and turning out more functional illiterates than ever before.

The world is in trouble, folks. And as one of tomorrow's leaders, it's up to you to move the world toward the light at the end of this long, dark tunnel.

Nobody else is going to do it for you. It is up to those of us who are already leaders. No one else has more at stake. No one else has better skills for rallying support, for setting agendas, for turning strategy into action, for making things happen, for challenging the status quo. You are the ones on whose shoulders this burden must fall.

The medicine we've got to swallow as part of the Ethics Epidemic includes this personal responsibility to become part of the solution to the many problems plaguing our society and our world.

We're all going to have to become activists. Our society once was replete with activists. While we trotted off to work, our briefcase and our Wall Street Journal tucked under our elbow, they fed the hungry and comforted the sick and saw to the needs of the elderly.

They were our volunteers. They were our wives and our mothers and our sisters. Today, they join us in the board room. And suddenly the labor pool for the volunteer movement that fueled this nation for so long has shrunk dramatically.

It's a cinch no one wants the women in the work force to pack up their desks and leave — they've brought far too much to our board rooms for us to be willing to give that up.

So we have to find another solution.

Shirt-Sleeves Effort

And here is the solution: Those of us who are the leaders in our professions are also going to have to become the leaders in our communities.

Certainly, there is great precedent for that. We chair committees. Business leaders with clout have always been in demand for prestigious boards and popular fund-raising efforts. But I believe we're also going to have to take a sleeves-rolled- up approach to the many ills that plague us.

It's got to be more than making donations to make sure we move into the right tax brackets. We're all going to have to get callouses on our hands. We're going to have to skin our knees.

When I was coming up, every role model I had was a role model of giving. Teachers, parents, church leaders, business leaders in the community. I grew up knowing that volunteerism was expected of me. It was important in the seasoning of the recipe.

I'm not sure the current generation is as strongly grounded in that kind of belief as we once were. Somewhere along the line, we cut off the spigot for a while. In 1968, we fought our generation of young people in the streets — when they had their own ideas about working for a better world — and perhaps that effectively killed the fire for involvement for a whole generation.

And now, for the past decade, we've seen another generation of youth become involved in the quest to keep up, to make more money, have more tangible things. The quest is so all-consuming that there isn't enough time left to do anything for anybody else.

It may be difficult to expect any other response from the generations that grew up knowing from infancy that mankind had the power to obliterate itself with the push of a button. How can we argue for delaying gratification when tomorrow may never arrive?

If we don't reverse that way of thinking now, we're facing much more than a nuclear time bomb. We're facing an ecological time bomb. An educational time bomb. Societal time bombs of drugs and poverty and the new racism and the simmering anger inherent in those problems.

We've got to stop listening to the tick and hoping someone else will find the fuse.

Influencing Quality of Life

"We're faced with picking up some of the job that our government used to do and is no longer going to do," said Hugh McColl, chairman of NCNB Corporation. "It has to do with social responsibilities both for our own employees and their families and the world around us. Those are the big challenges of the '90s and we have to meet them."

Business people sometimes get so caught up in hurrying to the next meeting and finishing the next report, American Express VP Linda Lockman-Brooks told The Charlotte Observer, that they forget their skills can be used to accomplish good things for other people.

Dr. Ruth Shaw, president of one of the largest and most respected community colleges in the nation, believes community involvement is even more important now than it was five years ago.

"Some of the people in our community are not only corporate leaders, but they are influential in the quality of life in this community," said Dr. Shaw, who became the first woman ever to chair the annual United Way effort in her community just four years after moving to town. "They bring the resources of their institutions to bear on the important issues in this community.

"The only way, really, for institutions to be a player is when leaders are both modeling and encouraging that kind of engaging in community issues."

An example of what she means? In Dr. Shaw's community, her college joined forces with the city government to provide its nationally-recognized literacy training to those who use the community's homeless shelter. The college works closely with the local school system to identify at-risk students and provide the parents of those at-risk students, when necessary, with free literacy training. The local power company is partner in a similar project for its employees.

In its special Tenth Anniversary Issue, Inc. magazine profiled a number of entrepreneurs, including Ben Cohen, half of the young team who founded Ben & Jerry's Homemade Inc., one of the most popular upscale ice cream companies in the country. Growing up in the '60s, Cohen said, he had the typical '60s attitude about mercenary business people.

"I'm a lot more aware of the power of business to act as a force for social change now," he concluded in the magazine.

Featured in that same issue was Yvon Chouinard, founder of the outdoor clothing company Patagonia Inc. He was ready to sell his business, he said, because he'd made enough money to live on for the rest of his life and didn't see the point in growing his business just for the sake of a bigger company.

"What turned me around was the discovery that I could use the company as a tool," Inc. quoted Chouinard.

He was being courted to locate Patagonia in a particular community and discovered that he could make demands for an improved ecology in the area. And his demands were met, simply because the community wanted his business.

"Through Patagonia, I could change things that I couldn't change on my own," he said. "I'd never before equated business with doing anything good, never thought of using it to promote a cause."

Chouinard, fearing that all the horror-story predictions about the environment were coming true, decided then and there to use his successful company to make the world a better place. Today, the only profits he pulls out of Patagonia go to environmental causes.

Jim Heavner sees a strong correlation between those who are successful within The Village Companies and their level of community spirit.

"Those managers who are most successful in achieving their goals within our company have also been those who have been most prominent in community leadership roles," Heavener said. "The ethics should be that you give according to your ability to give.

"The more you have been blessed with opportunity, the greater the responsibility you have to give something back."

Heavner helped start a project called the public-private partnership, a leadership consortium for finding ways to improve the community.

Harvey Gantt, a Charlotte architect, also feels strongly that business leaders are going to have to bring their skills to other arenas, to solve problems other than profit margins and sales quotas. Gantt puts his money where his mouth is. He was Charlotte's first Black mayor. And he recently ran for U.S. Senate against a long-entrenched encumbent.

"America needs to take advantage of this opportunity of relaxation of tension in the world to finally start to look a little bit more closely at its own resources, its own habits, its own values," Gantt said. "That's one of the very reasons I ran for U.S. Senate."

Because he wants to be part of the solution.

Looking Inward

The problems that need solutions are many. Leaders

like Dr. Tom Haggai with IGA and Tom Carpenter with
Aetna and John Fox with Bostik and Dieter Tannenberg
with Sargent-Welch Scientific Company and Jim Babb,
now with Outlet Television, agree that the biggest problem U.S. society faces may be education.

"American business has got to get involved with public
education," Carpenter said. "The quality of public education is lower than it should be. Government can't do it."

Fox encourages people to look at Lee Iacocca's strong
advocacy for the literacy movement.

"Reading is a skill that's vital for anything you want to
do, whether you want to be a poet, an artist, a mathemati-
cian or a rocket scientist," Fox said. "I believe education
is the best place to put our energy rather than asking
American industry to train people after the fact."

The station where I spent most of my broadcast career,
WBT- AM and WBTV in Charlotte, belongs to Jefferson-Pilot Communications, a company that has built a
reputation for community service.

Just in Charlotte, the radio and TV affiliates have
raised more than a half-million dollars for children's
health charities through a program called Penny Pitch.
They work with the local Arts and Science Council. They
sponsor fund-raisers for the United Negro College Fund.

And because former President Jim Babb took seriously
the indicators that say skilled employees are going to be
hard to find in the decade ahead, they formed a partnership with an elementary school which has a high percentage of disadvantaged children — minorities, kids from
single-parent homes. More than 70 Jefferson-Pilot
employees volunteer as tutors, as lunch pals, to organize
Christmas parties or field trips, even financial assistance
for the children at this school.

"The educators feel we're having a meaningful impact on the children, improving both their self-esteem and their skills like reading," Babb said. "And it's one of the greatest morale boosters we've ever done. The employees love it. Last summer, I was on an elevator with one of our employees and she said she couldn't wait for school to start back. She missed the children."

Babb also made sure Jefferson-Pilot employees were involved in their own children's schools. Everyone could take time off for teacher conferences, PTA meetings, even lunch in the school cafeteria.

"These are things that companies can and should do," Babb said. "We can't just continue to demand better products out of the schools without making some effort ourselves. Clearly, education is a national concern and it's too big a problem to leave it up to our educators to worry about.

"It's going to take a major investment of resources. Not just money, but involvement and interest and awareness."

Gantt pointed out that people are beginning to recognize that the quality of education may be as important as the quality of the products being produced by American business.

"The new competitiveness that is going to occur worldwide forces us to look inward at our own resources," he said. "It's going to force us, not just because we have some idealistic love of education, but because the very survival of our businesses may depend on it."

Are we prepared to handle the changes that will come because of the changes in the European community, Gantt wants to know. Are we prepared for the influx of minorities expected from South America and Central America? Are we prepared to train people? Are we prepared to keep up?

"Public education needs to be supported by businesses," Gantt said. "In their willingness to pay additional taxes to improve the system; their willingness to contribute their talents to help public school systems improve the quality of graduates; their willingness to provide summer jobs and an orientation into the world of work.

"There are a whole lot of things I have not always seen businesses appear to be as vigorous about."

Dr. Shaw agrees with Jim Babb that the problems education faces need solutions other than money and taxes.

"Education needs help in terms of expertise," she said. "Help us get technology into the schools, to the extent that we can really train people for the world that awaits them."

One of her college's solutions is a new Advanced Technology Center, supported through partnerships with companies such as IBM, Kodak-Verbatim and Okuma. The partnerships provide up-to-date equipment for training in the technologies — equipment that would be out of reach with the budget provided by state and county tax money. The partnerships give the businesses the opportunity to help establish the kind of training they need for new employees and to draw new employees from the pool of students and current graduates. Students get state-of-the-art training and, in many cases, on-the-job training.

Everyone wins.

The Commission on the Skills of the American Work Force recently completed a report, "America's Choice: High Skills or Low Wages." The report called on business, schools and government to overhaul training. Specifically, it recommended:

• Federal requirements that all U.S. businesses

devote 1% of their payroll to skills training;

- Mandates that people younger than 18 cannot hold jobs unless they meet a new set of educational standards that are as tough as any in the world; and
- Establishing a network of "youth centers" to help drop-outs, adding an estimate that $8 billion a year would be needed to help all current drop-outs.

Tough solutions to a problem that won't get any easier if we continue to ignore it. Without a doubt, it's time we all started thinking like Hugh McColl, who sees it as his bank's responsibility to improve the schools in his area with both volunteer help and money.

"We believe our business should be deeply involved in trying to improve the standards in our schools, to improve the environment in which young kids are growing up so they have a better chance of making it through high schools and getting an education," he said.

McColl isn't just sweet-talking, either. He's granted each of his 30,000 employees two hours a week to work with their own and other children in their local schools. That's 60,000 hours a week company-wide. You add it up.

Companies like Aetna, to combat a shortage of qualified workers, have also tackled the problem by taking on the challenge of educating its own workers.

"Aetna committed to build an employee education center," Carpenter said. "It cost close to $50 million — that is really plowing something into your future and taking the long-term view. But we realized that the whole area of employees — recruiting, training and developing employees — is what really sets this company apart."

Marvin Citron recommends that employers get "education-friendly." In other words, if I work for you and you know I've got six kids in school, let me know that you support me in taking time off to visit the schools and work with my kids. In other words, be a direct part of the solution at the grass roots level.

Follow Your Heart

Education may be, in the minds of some, the most important place for business leaders to become involved. But there are other ways and other areas in which to be involved. Let's look at some of the best examples from around the country.

• **Home Town Proud** — IGA has centered an entire advertising campaign around the concept of community spirit and involvement.

"We encourage our 3,000 stores in 48 states to be proud of their community, to do things for the community, to be givers," said Haggai.

• **Mad Dads** — John Foster, a Black father in Omaha, has taken to the streets with other fathers to provide role models for youth in trouble, as well as working with and protecting youth who are not.

High school principal Thomas Harvey was quoted in The Charlotte Observer as saying, "I think that many of us watched what was going on in our community and thought, 'How can I help?' Suddenly, it was there...When the Mad Dads were formed, I sensed a kind of sigh of relief from the kids. Somebody cared."

Patricia Alford Williams, an editorial writer for the Pulitzer-winning Observer, concluded, "Mad Dads may not be the answer for every community where young people are a prominent force in violent crimes. But statistics show when young people have caring and nurturing adults in their lives, they are much less likely to get involved in crime, drugs or other anti-social behavior.

"...It may not be enough now for caring adults to just take responsibility for our own children. We may have to give time and energy to young people who don't have good role models at home."

Certainly, there is power in that kind of one-on-one commitment.

• **National Foundation for Teaching Entrepreneurship to Handicapped and Disadvantaged Youth Inc.** — Steve Mariotti is another success story from Inc. magazine's special issue. After being mugged by young people in New York, Mariotti asked himself if young people would turn to petty crime if they could be shown a better way. It became an obsession.

Thinking back over his own experiences, Mariotti realized he had turned his life around by starting his own company. That experience, he realized, had boosted his self-esteem and gave him a feeling of control over his life. Why, he reasoned, wouldn't it work for disadvantaged youth?

In short order, Mariotti had young people filling out sole- proprietorship forms and printing business cards. They wrote business plans. They registered their businesses. Within weeks, street-smart kids were talking and acting like Harvard MBAs.

"Whether these kids build up a Ford Motor Co. or something like that has always been secondary to me," Mariotti was quoted. "What's important is the sentence structure that's going on in their minds. It can be a can-do sentence structure, and then everything else falls into place.

"As they become stronger mentally they become much better people. It's not a cure-all, but it's a small part — definitely an important part — of a solution to the problems of the inner city."

• **Mentor Program, the Bankers Educational Society Inc. (BESI) of North Carolina** — This 250-member minority bankers group has put together a program with the goal of preparing minority students for banking careers.

Charlotte banker Georgia McLean, one of the mentors, was also one of the first group of students with BESI mentors. "I've taken them shopping to get their business attire," she told The Charlotte Observer. "I take them to dinner to get them used to having a dinner interview. I tell them what fork to use, because sometimes they don't know."

Seminars on how to handle job interviews, effective resumes and achieving success are part of the program.

• **Habitat for Humanity** — Former President Jimmy Carter has certainly put his principles to work with this project, which helps low income families take part in building their own homes. Volunteers have built thousands of Habitat communities and Carter has been out there pounding nails with everyone else.

Mae Douglas with Ciba-Giegy made the point that her company sees this kind of commitment and involvement as part of its business ethics.

"When you mention our name in town, it always gets attention," she said. "I believe that's because our people are involved. Our people have a commitment to this community. There's a strong interest in making sure that, as a corporate citizen, we're doing our best to make this a good place to live."

Working in broadcast at WBT-WBTV in Charlotte, as I did for many years, part of the philosophy was that we gave back to the community. We owed our success to that community, and our community efforts were attempts to give something back in return, at least in small measure.

During my years at WBT-WBTV, there were many days when I spent eight hours on the job followed by eight hours doing some kind of community service work.

Where you expend your effort is up to you. In the same way that you look for work that puts fire in your belly, you'll want to give your community service to something which empassions you. The choices are up to you.

But whatever your personal choice, don't fail to work for it. The time has come for all of us to add that back to our individual measure of success. The time for taking only has passed; we're going to have to give back to our world.

NEXT: Customer Service

"*Listen, listen, listen.*"

- Ross Perot
As quoted in
Fortune magazine

SERVICE: OUR MOST IMPORTANT PRODUCT

10

Join me, for just a moment, in a study in contrasts.

A colleague of mine recently planned a conference with a local hotel. It wasn't a big conference — only about 40 people from around the state. She ironed out all the details with the hotel's conference coordinator months ahead of time, and followed up several times at different stages.

As a final precaution, she called her contact at the hotel the day before just to make sure everyone was clear on all the details. She even asked if it would help for her to be there when the meeting room was set up, in case there were any questions.

"That's not necessary," she was told. "We have the floor plan right here and I've gone over everything with the man who'll do the set-up."

My colleague arrived early Saturday morning anyway. And lucky she did. The man had just finished setting up the room — with only two tables and four chairs.

My friend finished setting up the room herself, with some assistance from the baffled hotel worker.

"I really expected to hear from my contact at the hotel first thing Monday morning," she told me. "I expected to hear profuse apologies and perhaps negotiate some kind of adjustment on our contract. I didn't hear from her. For two weeks, I didn't hear from her.

"When she finally called, it was to express concern that I hadn't paid for the facility the day of the conference, as agreed."

What's most interesting to me is that my friend didn't get angry at the mismanagement or the nonchalant attitude — she said it's about what she's come to expect. It was only when the conference coordinator at the hotel said, "Well, it wasn't my fault," that my colleague decided that no amount of adjustment on the financial arrangements of her contract would ever convince her to do business with that hotel again.

That's one story about service. Here is another.

About three years ago, I had scheduled a training session for AT&T in Williamsburg, Va., one evening and another in Murphreesboro, Tenn., the next morning. It wasn't until I started looking at flight connections that I realized what a problem I'd created — I had to charter a plane in order to keep both commitments.

Hoping to keep things running as smoothly as possible, my office had called the Wayside Inn in Murphreesboro to let them know I would arrive late — very late.

When my plane arrived at 2 a.m., I was more than a little amazed to find that a cab awaited my arrival — thanks to the thoughtfulness of the folks at the Wayside Inn.

When my cab arrived at the hotel, not only had they saved my room for me, but manager David Gillam also had been thoughtful enough to leave a snack in the refrigerator in my room — a sandwich, slice of pie and fruit.

Total bill for my stay: $28.90! You couldn't have bought that kind of service for ten times that much.

This was not the Ritz Carlton. But it was so friendly and warm you would have sworn you'd just been set down in your favorite aunt's house. That's how well the Wayside Inn cared for me. Little wonder the Wayside Inn is always full and David Gillam is a hero among his peers.

We hardly need to discuss the contrast between my experience and my friend's experience. I don't have to point out to you where you would be more inclined to do repeat business, if you were the customer.

I probably don't even have to point out to you that, in the heavily competitive world of the future, you won't be alone in taking your business to the Wayside Inns of the world. And that the not-so-subtle differences in the two businesses are likely to translate into not-so-subtle differences in the bottom line, as well.

The difference is service. Real service. Not lip service. The kind of "just do it" service that everybody has talked about for the past decade, but few have actually delivered. The kind of service that is so exceptional that it draws attention to itself, while service that is so poor it constitutes no service at all has become the norm.

Greeting customers with a smile. Keeping your facilities spotlessly clean. Acknowledging customers as quickly as possible, not long after they've despaired of ever getting any help. Taking the blame when anything goes wrong and being committed to making it right — no matter what.

"We have to understand the needs of our customers just as if they were our own needs and adopt those needs, internalize them," said John Fox. "Reflect that right back to the customer. Let them know we understand their needs and that we have every bit of energy in our organization trying to respond to those needs."

It all sounds so basic. Things we all know. Yet, they are the very things that get ignored in our efforts to do other things — improve the technology, up the numbers of sales calls, lower absenteeism.

Ignoring such service is part of what Tom Peters calls TDC — Thinly Disguised Contempt for the customer.

"It's the biggest barrier to superior performance — in hospitals, schools, retailers, or manufacturing companies — that exists in America today," Peters wrote in "Common Courtesy: The Ultimate Barrier to Entry."

For the decade ahead, the kind of service you deliver is going to determine what kind of profits you earn. It will determine how loyal your customers are. How likely you are to be opening your doors for business again next year.

"Those companies who focus on other goals, such as purely financial goals with no attention to quality and customer service — those are companies that are going to suffer," said Dieter Tannenberg.

Service will become a measure of success. Because it only takes one competitor whose main product is service and you'll feel the effects on your bottom line.

"There are lots of businesses in the U.S. where quality is going to become more important than volume," said Tom Carpenter. "More companies are going to take the position that they want to be the best rather than the biggest."

The best, not necessarily the biggest. Unless you're going to be in the lowest bidder business, you'd better be in the service business.

And if you plan to be in the lowest bidder business, be

vigilant. Somebody else can always do it cheaper. Loyalty does not exist in the marketplace of the lowest bidder.

Loyalty is bought with service. "We always want to exceed what our customers thought they were getting when they bargained for it in the first place," said Jim Heavner. "They won't ever quit you if you give them more than they thought they were going to get."

So let's discuss the reasons for the differences in my friend's experience and mine — and how your organization can become the Wayside Inn of your industry.

And not an organization that is more concerned with placing blame somewhere else than it is in satisfying the customer.

Employees Are the Key

The next time I have to be within a 50-mile radius of Murphreesboro, Tenn., I'll go out of my way to stay at the Wayside Inn.

The reason is the service and that difference is possible because of the employees who deliver the service. So the trick is in figuring out how you, as the leader, can coax the Wayside Inn attitude out of your employees.

But the trick is really no trick at all. The answer is simple. But it isn't often done.

The trick is in how your company treats its employees. Because the way you treat your employees is the way your employees will treat your customers.

The way you make your employees feel is the way your employees will make your customers feel.

Given the morale in most companies in the U.S., that could be one of the most frightening realizations a leader can come to. It also points up the significance of all the team-building strategies we discussed in Chapters Three, Four and Five.

The bond you build with your co-workers is a bond that will be extended to your customers.

In a 1988 Piedmont Airlines (now USAir) magazine profile of J.W. Marriott, Jr., the hotel and restaurant magnate talked about nurturing his people, acknowledging they are his greatest resource. The results of that nurturing came through in a story he recounted about a business traveler who washed his hands right before leaving his room to check out — forgetting the wedding ring he had left beside the sink.

A bellboy, Marriott said, drove to the airport and hunted the traveler down to return the ring.

"It's those little things that aren't in the policy manual that mean good service," Marriott said.

He's right. And some businesses are now even going so far as to put some of them in the policy manuals. I've seen examples of that in some automobile dealerships these days. The auto industry is one of the most competitive businesses out there right now. Everyone is scratching and clawing to survive. And the smart ones are realizing that the best way to survive is by delivering the best service.

The first step is in empowering employees — giving them authority to make decisions. Telling them they are important enough to make a decision and that decision will be backed up by the company.

A couple of years back, USA Today reported that both Ford Motor Company and General Motors Corporation would allow dealers to authorize repairs on out-of-warranty vehicles. The story quoted a parts and service director at a dealership in Orlando, discussing a customer whose power windows had failed on a three-year-old Lincoln Town Car. The car was no longer under warranty and the customer was riled.

Because he had been empowered to send away satisfied customers, the service manager did just that. He made the repairs. No charge.

Less than two weeks later, the customer's brother came in and bought a wagon. A week later, another relative bought a Town Car.

The two cars sold for close to $50,000. A pretty good return on the investment of a couple hundred dollars in good service.

So empowerment of employees is one key. But don't forget that it goes deeper than that. Happy employees equal happy customers. That sounds too simplistic to be realistic, but it's true. An employee who feels good about coming to work is going to be there with a smile for the customer.

And the customer will respond to that employee before the customer will respond to the best discount you offer. Amway's Dexter Yager puts it this way: "Customers first buy a sales person before they buy the product. The person makes all the difference."

More than Banners, Buttons

Now that we understand what is at the heart of genuine service, let's take a look at the logistics of making that happen.

We've all seen or heard of attempts to fire up a company and generate better service. A big campaign is launched. Every employee gets a button. A banner is hung in the employee cafeteria, heralding the slogan. And for a few weeks, a few months, everyone is fired up. Everyone is conscious of customer needs. Everyone bends over backward to make the customer happy.

Then, one day, the enthusiasm for bending over backward begins to wane. Somebody comes in tired. Or disgruntled. The banner in the cafeteria, if it's still there, is just a bit frayed and a bit droopy — like the spirit behind it.

That's human nature. We lose our zeal. The fire burns out. And the "customer is king" mentality becomes an echo from the past.

But service is not slogans and buttons and smiling when you feel like it. Service is something we do all the time. Regardless. It is a standard we set and then pursue. Relentlessly. It's not a program that you start and stop. It's an ongoing process, one that continues even when the hooplah stops and we're suddenly on the bandwagon behind another buzz word.

Service must become as much a part of the procedure as sending out invoices or keeping vacation records or making sure you fulfill all your obligations to Uncle Sam's boys at the IRS.

How do you do that? Here's the step-by-step procedure for setting in motion a service plan at your organization. It's no different, you'll see, than the procedure you'd use if you suddenly had need for another layer of paperwork or a new process for approving raises.

It's just another process. But it may be the most important process you set in motion.

1. Plan strategies that are concrete. Make sure

your goals are specific and your progress can be measured.

2. Get enthusiastic buy-in from the people who can make or break it — the employees who will implement it.
3. Make sure everyone who will be involved understands the benefits of successfully carrying out the program.
4. Seek input from everyone. Brainstorm. Listen.
5. Clearly make specific people responsible for specific parts of the program.
6. Make sure you're aiming at short-term goals and long-term goals.
7. Set up a timeline for implementing the program, including an official start-up date.
8. Measure your results.
9. Listen, listen, listen.

Let's take those one at a time and discuss them in a bit more detail.

• *Plan strategies that are concrete.* Don't say, "We're committed to satisfying our customers." Say, as Tom Gould at Younkers did, "We're empowering all of our employees to say 'Yes' to our customers. We're empowering all of our employees to solve the customers' problems at the first point of contact."

Or say, as First Union Bank said, "We now have a sundown rule. Any customer who comes in with a problem will have some kind of response by sundown."

Or say, as did Stew Leonard, famous grocer in Norwalk, Connecticut, "We'll have a customer focus group every Saturday, to find out what's bugging our customers. Then we'll fix those problems and post the solutions in a prominent place, so our customers will know we're listening to them." Measurable plans, not platitudes.

• *Get enthusiastic buy-in from employees.* We've already agreed that the heart of successful service is the person delivering that service. So, once you've decided on the direction you're going, you must create as broad a base of delivery for your program as possible. And that means including everyone — not just the middle-management, not just the supervisors, everyone — in the entire process. In planning. In setting objectives. In the continuing search for ways to do it better.

And how do you manage that? First, by making sure you're already living by Chapters Three through Five. Second, by remembering steps three, four and five in your implementation plan.

• *Sell the benefits to everyone.* We're all subject to the "What's In It For Me?" rule. Even employees must be sold on the idea that there's something to be gained from following through on the actions in your plan. And you should, if you've developed a concrete, well-thought-through plan, be able to tell everyone in some very specific ways what the value of your new service program is.

Will it be financial incentives for those with more repeat business over a specific period of time? Will it be a higher percentage of profit-sharing for all? Higher profits company wide, with the increased stability that often comes with greater profits? Or an investment in the new technology everyone knows you need but can't afford to put in the budget yet? Will it be greater opportunities as business expands? Will it be greater individual automony as employees at all levels are empowered to do their jobs?

• *Make sure your employees know what they stand to gain.* Seek input. Brainstorm with employees. Work at their sides for a week. Ask the front-line employees and the assembly-line workers and the plant operations people what it would take to do their job better. To create a climate for serving customers better. To offer a higher quality product.

Do everything you can to get employees at every level to bring their ideas to the floor. Then use those ideas. They'll be better ideas than you'll get from a bunch of upper-echelon types who don't roll up their sleeves every day.

• *Define who's responsible.* Giving people the authority to carry out a project gives both ownership and accountability. Make sure everyone understands what is expected and has the resources to carry out what is expected.

• *Set up short-term goals and long-term goals.* Know where you're going, how you plan to get there and how long it's going to take to get there. Know what you can expect to accomplish in three months, in six months, in five years.

And make sure those objectives are expressed, again, in measurable, concrete ways. Don't set out to increase repeat business. Set out to increase your percentage of repeat business from 2 percent to 10 percent. In the first year.

That's an objective, not a pipe dream.

• *Set up a timetable.* It's another way to be specific and measurable. If we know that planning runs through June and everything kicks off on July 1, with a major ad campaign or the landing of a hot air balloon in the parking lot or the completion of an intensive training program or the infusion of an extra $100,000 into the budget, then the steps to which we are committed take on urgency, immediacy.

If we shake hands at the end of a planning session and walk away in agreement to, "Get this thing started

ASAP," everybody's too fuzzy about what happens next to really make anything happen.

• *Check your progress*. Another part of this business of being concrete. You know what you're trying to do, so find a way to make sure you're doing it. Use statistics. Use company records. Establish a feedback system. Plan a series of focus groups at regular intervals. Make sure you know your benchmarks, then measure your progress against those benchmarks.

• *Listen, listen, listen*. That's Ross Perot's advice and you can't beat it. Every day, listen. To customers. To competitors. To employees. To the people who used to be your customers.

Remember, service is an ongoing process. And unless you keep your ears open, you'll never know when that process needs a little tinkering.

Plenty of bumps in the road lie ahead as you move toward a do-able plan for making service your number one product. Your employees may be leery of yet another big project. They may wonder how much extra work will fall on their shoulders, with nothing to show for it. You may have trouble getting different departments to work together.

You see the common denominator in each of these problem areas, don't you? They're all people problems. Every single one of them is related to how successfully you build and motivate and manage your team.

Part of the Equation

I want to talk about one more element of service, an element that is separate at the same time it is integral to the kind of service we've been discussing.

Quality. Without quality, there is no service. Without service, there is no quality.

To put things in their simplest terms, I define quality in terms of product and service in terms of people. Quality is achieved when you've delivered the best product you can deliver, made of the best materials by the most conscientious workers, made to be durable and safe and worth the dollars paid for it.

Service is delivered when you back up that product with a satisfaction-guaranteed attitude, with assistance delivered cheerfully and not grudgingly, with attention to problems that is prompt and courteous and at least one mile beyond what is expected.

Quality and service. Hand in glove. And both too often forgotten during the past decades. "Quality was clearly on the decline for about 10 years," said John Fox. "Fortunately, American industry now understands that we're going down the wrong road. Initially, we were simply reacting to Japan's penetration into the U.S. markets. Just trying to respond to that loss of market share.

"But in doing that, many companies adopted more stringent quality control — a new philosophy in the way they run their business and a source of pride for their companies.

Ross Perot, in telling Fortune magazine how he would turn around General Motors, spoke first of quality.

"Starting today, in order to build the finest cars in the world, GM will listen to its customers, listen to its dealers who sell the cars to customers, listen to the men and women who assemble its cars in the factories, and listen to the engineers who design its cars," he said. "The watchword will be: 'Listen, listen, listen.' ... Their ideas, fresh from the marketplace, will make GM the best in the world."

So listen, listen, listen, if you want to make your product, whatever it is, the best in the world.

NEXT: Big Changes, Small Changes

"Every recession we've had since World War II has been preceded by some major shock to consumer confidence, whether it be an embargo, an assassination or something — something dramatic."

- John Fox
Bostik

SHOOTING THE JEEP DRIVER AND OTHER TOOLS FOR TOMORROW

11

Business bonding. A return to service. Embracing diversity. Coaching the individual.

Some of the best leaders I've had the good fortune to work with during my years as a trainer have shared some terrific ideas for making the Ethics Epidemic a reality in the decade ahead.

For our final chapter, what I'd like to do is pull together some of their scattershot comments about the trends that will affect us as we head to the 21st century.

What will global competition mean to us? How can we cope with a workplace that may ask us to lead one company today and a different company tomorrow? What role will women really play in the decade ahead? And the aging worker?

And, from our friend Robert Stark with Hallmark, one final thought that will help us put it all in perspective.

Toppling the King of the Hill

Everyone interviewed for this book acknowledged the impact global competition will have on our economy in the decade ahead. Some see it as an exhilarating challenge.

Others feel the U.S. is already a couple of laps behind in the race for economic dominance.

"As a country, we're going to have to come to grips with a number of fundamental things," said Robert Stark with Hallmark Cards. "We're not the kingpins of the world economy as we were subsequent to World War II, all through the '50s, '60s and maybe early '70s. Our markets are not necessarily going to be ever-expanding for us, so we're going to have to fight for whatever it is we get."

Stark feels that the biggest obstacle to facing this challenge is the fact that not everyone understands or believes the magnitude of the problem.

"We were king of the hill for 30 years, with constantly expanding markets and a world full of shortages," he said. "That has changed rather rapidly. That's a profound change and it happened very rapidly."

To stop the economic erosion that Stark feels has already begun, we must understand and accept the challenge and collectively decide to tackle it.

"Americans don't have the God-given right to the highest standard of living in the world," Stark said. "And I believe a lot of our people perhaps don't understand that."

Jim Heavner with The Village Companies backed up Stark's assertion that global competition is going to require much more than just one company working to outsell its international competitors. He pointed out that the Japanese, for example, have been aided not only by the Japanese work ethic, but also by the government's economic policy.

"You can trace it back to the '50s," Heavner said, "when the government developed national economic policies to promote those industries that were seen as potentially competitive.

"If we were to attempt that in this country, there would be a lot of political debate about a managed economy. Clearly, the ability to coalesce the people behind those policies is going to be important."

And it's going to be important, most leaders agree, because success is going to be measured on a global scale.

"It's no longer possible to think about being a regional company or even a national company," said John Fox with Bostik. "You have to think in terms of being an international company, otherwise someone somewhere is going to beat you.

"What's going to emerge out of that is a challenge to companies to be the fastest, the most responsive and the smartest. The race here will not necessarily be won by the strongest, you also have to be the fastest and the most clever."

Not the strongest. But the fastest and the most clever. That means we must sacrifice something near and dear to the heart of American big business. Our layers of bureaucracy.

Rightsizing

If might no longer makes right in a global economy, what will make for global competitiveness?

John Fox recommends minimizing layers of management in hopes of maximizing the chances for honest-to-goodness communication. Global communication will see tremendous innovation in the next few years, he said.

But if filtering through layers of bureaucracy is a part of the problem, the solutions lie in more than improved communications technology.

Downsizing — cutting the fat from companies in an effort to cut fat from budgets — is a trend that we won't be leaving behind in the '80s. Only now we'll have another purpose in mind — it's our route to being the fastest and most clever.

"Organizations are going to downsize more than they have already," said Chris Hegerty. "It's going to be an exquisite time for small, flexible, entrepreneurial companies."

But experts already see one problem with downsizing. Most companies are approaching the process from the wrong end. They cut employees without a strategy. And the result is sometimes called Survivor Blues — fewer people growing discouraged and dissatisfied because they're being asked to do the same amount of work with less people-power. Couple that with the inevitable feelings of insecurity that follow when staffing is cut and you've done anything but improve productivity.

So how do you manage the need for trimming the fat? Make sure you're working from a well-planned strategy. First, decide what work you can afford to do without. Do your purchasing procedures require three layers of approval and eighteen kinds of paperwork? Are your decision-makers spending more time in meetings than they are in action?

Find out where you can cut the work expected, then

match the people you have to the work that is necessary. Then you can downsize — or "rightsize," as some are calling it — without creating a new layer of morale problems that will zap the productivity of the people left behind.

Another barrier to productivity, said Fox, is organizational barriers.

"In some companies, going from one department to another is like going from one planet to another," he said. "It's my objective to make sure in this business you can move from one aspect of the organization to another very, very easily.

"I just finished a discussion with one of our production operators who manufacturers apoxey resins. He was having a problem and wanted to talk about it. Organizationally, that person is five or six layers removed from where I am, but it doesn't matter. I try to keep that attitude prevalent."

Economic Cheerleading

No matter what trends impact our economy in the decade ahead, Fox sees one factor that can override any negative factors — and undermine any good ones.

Consumer confidence. As consumer confidence goes, said Fox, so goes the economy.

"If consumers are confident, then they are buying durable goods," Fox said. "Businesses are investing in new plants and equipment, upgrading their operation. If confidence is high, then in general economic conditions are good.

"Every recession we've had since World War II has been preceded by some major shock to consumer confidence, whether it be an embargo, an assassination or something — something dramatic."

Keeping consumer confidence high — serving as what Fox calls a confidence cheerleader — should therefore be one of the principal jobs of the president of our country, he said.

I have to agree — and it's one of yours as an organizational leader, as well.

Blind Faith and Clear Vision

One of the things that most of tomorrow's leaders will have to face is mobility. We're not going to be in the same place, leading the same people to the same goals for years on end. We'll be moving up and moving on. We'll change jobs and reach for greater challenges.

As leaders, how do we make sure that the problems that come with moving on remain challenges and not crises?

Lloyd Mahaffey, who had filled key positions with Apple, Honeywell and PCA before reaching his mid-30s, said that many times new leaders are brought in to solve the problems created by the old leaders.

"Most leaders have about 90 days of a honeymoon in an organization," said Mahaffey, one-time vice president of marketing for Commodore Computers and currently President of Start, Inc. "In that time, you've got to determine what some of the key problems are. You have to assess very carefully what's going on in the organization and you have to move quite swiftly to make changes."

But, Mahaffey cautioned, your moves have to make sense to the organization.

"To some degree, you have to get them to operate on faith and you simultaneously have to articulate a vision, so they understand what they're trying to get to," he said. "Then you can begin moving them beyond their desire to maintain the status quo."

Mahaffey also believes in doing something very visible and very symbolic during that 90-day honeymoon, to demonstrate to those who would follow you that you do, indeed, intend to lead them somewhere.

"Sometimes you have to shoot the jeep driver," he said. "What I mean by that is every once in a while you've got to knock off that one object that probably won't impact the organization substantially but is still highly visible, so everybody goes, 'Ooh, look at that change!'"

Entrenched management and its desire to protect past decisions is another problem faced by the new leader in an organization — especially when you know you've been brought in to cure the present ills.

"Where those past decisions were very poor, you acknowledge that," Mahaffey said. "Otherwise you lose credibility. You say, 'We're not going to do that any more.'

"At the same time, you give the management team credit for bringing the organization to the point that it is, so they're allowed to keep some self-esteem in the process."

In addition to the symbolism of shooting the jeep driver, Mahaffey believes in using positive symbolism to demonstrate that a new day is at hand.

"One of the things I always try to do when I come to a new organization is to build a new logo and a new image for the organization," he said. "It's a way of shaking off the old and accepting the new. It sort of allows you to buff up a tarnished piece of brass, if you will.

"It gives everybody something new to focus on and it

also gives you a chance to develop a whole new set of performance standards around the new image."

Then, he puts that new symbolism to work by passing out t-shirts or caps or buttons bearing the new symbol. And that effort can be a subtle way of gaining a slight degree of buy-in, he pointed out.

Because once your employees have accepted the gift of the t-shirt, along with its symbolism that things have changed, they have taken the first important step toward beginning to accept the changes behind that symbol, too.

Population Changes

We've already heard an economist with one of the country's leading banks say that the major story of the decade ahead will be demographics. The labor pool will shrink and women will constitute the majority. You won't be allowed to forget those trends, because you're going to see the effects.

"One difference, I think, is that there is going to be less pressure on the aging population to retire," Tom Carpenter said.

It's a trend, he said, that Americans are just beginning to acknowledge, but one that has been at work in other parts of the world for a long time. From Churchill to DeGaulle, he pointed out, senior members of society have long been in demand for their wisdom. And as that part of our population grows in number and remains healthy longer, expect to see more character lines on the faces of those who are calling the shots.

Another emerging force is women. "The women who have been coming up in corporate America for the last 15 years are really going to pop out through the top in the '90s," Carpenter said. "Women are a great resource for American business which has not been utilized to its highest capacity."

His warning to those women is not to forget the harsh reality that women still have to work harder and at consistently higher levels of performance in order to be the the achievers. He encourages women to seek mentors and to serve as mentors, and to be realistic about the obstacles that still exist.

"Because there are obstacles," Carpenter said. "Women in businesses which have been historically dominated by men just aren't permitted to make the mistakes. Mistakes by women are remembered. So you have to know that and not make the mistakes."

Astronaut Linda Godwin pointed out that, even though it's almost routine to find women involved in this country's space program, women still need to remember that integrating women into the workplace is still in progress and not an accomplished fact.

"What really has to happen is more women going into math and science and engineering," Godwin said. "So I like to encourage that in grade school, junior high and high school. That kind of interest has to be developed. And all that has to happen before you can see women really coming into their own in this kind of world."

I have to agree with people like Knight-Ridder's Dot Ridings, who feels that women bring some terrific assets to the business world. The differences aren't in our chromosomes, she said, but in our upbringing and our life experiences.

"A lot of the people skills that are so critical to good leadership tend to come more naturally to women than they do to men," she said. "We are taught, by and large, to be good listeners, to be sympathetic and empathetic. We are trained to be people-oriented and interested in other people.

"Women can bring a tremendous strength to our business world."

Enjoy the Journey

An important quality of leadership, certainly, is vision — being able to see where you want to go and how you need to go about getting there. But Robert Stark with Hallmark sees another important element.

"Joy plays into it somewhere. We ought to enjoy the journey," he said. "We too often concentrate on finishing, getting there and getting it done instead of concentrating on the joy of the journey. It's just like most of our trips — the destination is not nearly as exciting as you thought it was going to be once you get there.

"We need to approach business and life that way, that the journey is the thing you ought to enjoy rather than the end result."

Joy. I can't think of a more positive note to end the journey we've taken into tomorrow's business world. I can't think of a better way to assure that we add value and integrity to our business dealings than by approaching it with joy. I can't think of a more certain way to infuse others with fire in the belly. I can't think of a better way to begin our journey toward the 21st Century.

I wish you success. I wish you joy.

Ty Boyd Enterprises, Incorporated
Board of Advisors

My close friends and professional advisors throughout the years. Their work is evident in this book, though I seem to get most of the credit.

Jim Babb, Broadcast CEO
Stuart Childs, Attorney
Anne Eddins, Accountant
Don Evans, Financial Advisor
Bill Hensley, PR Consultant
Bob Gilley, Insurance Executive
Jack King, Retailer
Bill Miller, Accountant
Van Weaterspoon, Developer
Joan Zimmerman, Promotions Executive

SPEAKERS ROUNDTABLE

Speakers Roundtable includes twenty-one of the nation's most prestigious speakers, trainers and consultants. They have served as friends, teachers and mentors. All are leaders in their professions.

Ken Blanchard	Escondido, California
Jim Cathcart	LaJolla, California
Danny Cox	Tustin, California
Patricia Fripp	San Francisco, California
Bill Gove	Atlantis, Florida
Tom Haggai	Chicago, Illinois/High Point, N.C.
Ira Hayes	Marco Island, Florida
Chris Hegarty	Novato, California
Art Holst	Peoria, Illinois
Allan Hurst	Palm Desert, California
Don Hutson	Memphis, Tennessee
Charles Jones	Mechanicsburg, Pennsylvania
Jim Newman	Studio City, California
Charles Plumb	Santa Barbara, California
Cavett Robert	Phoenix, Arizona
Murray Raphel	Atlantic City, New Jersey
Brian Tracy	Solana Beach, California
Herb True	South Bend, Indiana
Jim Tunney	Carmel-By-The-Sea, California
Tom Winninger	Waterloo, Iowa
Ty Boyd	Charlotte, North Carolina

_____ Yes, I'd like more information on the following resource material for myself or others in my organization:

_____ Additional copies of VISIONS

_____ Show and Sell (6 audio cassettes)

_____ Life Planning and Success Achievement (6 audio cassettes)

_____ Achievement Through Motivation Series (6 audio cassettes)

_____ Encyclopedia of Self-Improvement: 4 Volumes (each volume 12 audio cassettes with M.R. Kopmeyer, narrated by Ty Boyd)

_____ Insights Into Excellence (hard cover volume featuring the best advice from the Speakers Roundtable)

_____ Executive Speakers Institute (information on two and one-half day intensive training session)

FROM:

NAME: _____

TITLE: _____

COMPANY: _____

ADDRESS: _____

_____

PHONE: _____

FAX: _____

FAX TO: TY BOYD ENTERPRISES, INC.
The Cullen Center
1727 Garden Terrace
Charlotte, NC 28203
Phone: 704-333-9999
FAX: 704-333-0207